# The Dramatic Records of

# Sir Henry Herbert

## Master of the Revels, 1623-1673

Henry Herbert

(Editor: Joseph Quincy Adams)

# Alpha Editions

This edition published in 2019

ISBN : 9789353800536

Design and Setting By
**Alpha Editions**
email - alphaedis@gmail.com

# THE DRAMATIC RECORDS

OF

## SIR HENRY HERBERT

MASTER OF THE REVELS, 1623–1673

EDITED BY

JOSEPH QUINCY ADAMS

CORNELL UNIVERSITY

NEW HAVEN: YALE UNIVERSITY PRESS
LONDON: HUMPHREY MILFORD
OXFORD UNIVERSITY PRESS
MDCCCCXVII

PRESS OF
THE NEW ERA PRINTING COMPANY
LANCASTER, PA.

TO

CLARK SUTHERLAND NORTHUP

AS A TOKEN OF ESTEEM

# PREFACE

The dramatic records of the Office of the Revels during the reigns of Edward VI, Mary, and Elizabeth have been admirably edited with full indexes and notes by Professor Albert Feuillerat; but the records of the Office during the reigns of James I, Charles I, and Charles II remain either unedited or scattered in miscellaneous volumes, none of which is indexed. Every scholar working in the field of the Tudor-Stuart drama must have felt the desirability of having these later records printed in a more accessible form.

In the present volume I have attempted to bring together the dramatic records of Sir Henry Herbert, during whose long administration the Office of the Revels attained the height of its power and importance. These records, most of them preserved through Herbert's own care, consist of his office-book, covering the period of 1622–1642, a few documents relating to the same period, and miscellaneous documents relating to the management of the Office after the Restoration.

Of these records unquestionably the most important is the office-book, 1622–1642. The original manuscript, freely consulted by Edmond Malone and George Chalmers in the closing years of the eighteenth century, has since disappeared, but the better part of it is extant in the form of quotations strewn through the various works of those two scholars. Strange to say, these quotations have not hitherto been brought together, organized, and indexed. Fleay, indeed, in his *History of the Stage* makes use of much of the material, and attempts to record Herbert's licenses of plays and notices of Court performances; but he does not always quote the exact language of Herbert, neglects to indicate the sources of his statements, fails to discover many entries, and is often inaccurate as to dates and other important facts. Moreover the absence of an index to his volume makes the use even of the limited material he has included difficult. I have attempted to give every quotation which Malone and Chalmers made from the office-book, and every statement which they profess to base upon their examination of the manuscript; and when the exact words of Herbert are used I have indicated this by marks of quotation. Certain documents of the period 1622–1642 I have added as an appendix to the office-book.

The miscellaneous documents of the period 1660–1670 throw a great deal of light upon the office-book, and upon the conduct of the Office during the reigns of James I and Charles I. And, of course, they are indispensable to the student of the Restoration drama.

I desire to acknowledge the courtesy of the University of Pennsylvania Library, the fortunate possessor of one of the eleven copies of Halliwell-Phillipps's *A Collection of Ancient Documents Respecting the Office of Master of the Revels*, for the loan of that important volume.

JOSEPH QUINCY ADAMS

ITHACA, NEW YORK,
March 24, 1917

# TABLE OF CONTENTS

# ABBREVIATIONS

*Apology.*—An Apology for the Believers in the Shakspeare-Papers, which were Exhibited in Norfolk-Street. [By George Chalmers.] London, 1797.

*B. C. E. D.*—A Biographical Chronicle of the English Drama, 1559–1642. By Frederick Gard Fleay. 2 vols. London, 1891.

*Collection.*—A Collection of Ancient Documents Respecting the Office of Master of the Revels, and Other Papers Relating to the Early English Theatre, from the Original Manuscripts Formerly in the Haslewood Collection. [By J. O. Halliwell-Phillipps.] London, 1870. [Eleven copies printed.]

*Documents.*—Documents Relating to the Office of the Revels in the Time of Queen Elizabeth. Edited with Notes and Indexes by Albert Feuillerat. Louvain, 1908.

*Epistolary Curiosities.*—Epistolary Curiosities; Series the First; Consisting of Unpublished Letters, of the Seventeenth Century, Illustrative of the Herbert Family. By Rebecca Warner. London, 1818.

*History of the Stage.*—A Chronicle History of the London Stage, 1559–1642. By Frederick Gard Fleay. London, 1890.

*Revels.*—Extracts from the Accounts of the Revels at Court, in the Reigns of Queen Elizabeth and King James I., from the Original Office Books of the Masters and Yeomen. By Peter Cunningham. London, 1842.

*S. A.*—A Supplemental Apology for the Believers in the Shakspeare-Papers. By George Chalmers. London, 1799.

*Var.*—The Plays and Poems of William Shakspeare, with the Corrections and Illustrations of Various Commentators. London, 1821. [Edited by James Boswell, and generally known as the Variorum Shakespeare. The Herbert entries I have collated with Malone's edition of Shakespeare, 1790.]

# INTRODUCTION

# INTRODUCTION

## I.  THE OFFICE OF THE REVELS

The Office of Master of the Revels came into existence as a result of the multiplication of masques,
shows, and plays at the Court of the pleasure-loving
sovereign Henry VIII.[1]  At first, so we are told, there
was no regular official to care for the royal entertainments; but the king "being disposed to pastime would
at one time appoint one person, at sometime another
. . . to set forth such devices as might be most agree-
able to the prince's expectation."[2]  Among the persons
whom Henry VIII thus temporarily appointed to the
position were the Earl of Essex, Lord Leonard Grey,
Henry Wentworth, Sir Anthony Browne, and Sir Henry
Guildford, all of them courtiers "such as for credit,
pleasant wit, and ability in learning, he thought meet"
to have charge of the revels.  Moreover, under the
general direction of "the Prince's taylor, having the
oversight of the workmanship," there grew up within
the royal household an organization—composed of
property-makers, painters, tailors, clerks of the wardrobe, and such like—to provide the necessary equip-
ment for the ever increasing masques, shows, and entertainments.  This organization "afterwards," so we are
informed, "was made an office, and certain of the king's
household servants appointed by patent to have care

[1] For the earlier history of the revels at Court see A. Feuillerat, *Le Bureau
des Menus-Plaisirs*, 1910, and E. K. Chambers, *Notes on the History of the
Revels Office*, 1906.
[2] *Of the First Institution of the Revels*, a manuscript history of the Office of
the Revels, written in 1572-3.  See Feuillerat, *Documents*, p. 5.

3

thereof," the chief of whom was known as "the Serjeant of the Revels."

In 1544 the king appointed to the position of permanent manager of the revels no less a person than Sir Thomas Cawarden, one of the gentlemen of the Court who was known to be "skillful and delighting in matters of device." Since, however, Cawarden "did mislyke to be tearmed a 'Serieant' because of his better countenance of roome and place, being of the Kinge's maiestie's privye chamber," he was granted the more dignified title of—

Magister Iocorum, Revelorum, et Mascorum omnium et singulorum nostrorum, vulgariter nuncupatorum Revelles and Maskes.[1]

"And so," wrote the earliest historian of the office, "became he by patent the first Master of the Revels."

His duties were "to have care" merely of the entertainments at the Court; he did not attempt to control the professional actors, or to exercise any jurisdiction over the dramatic amusements of the general public. In this limited capacity he served with credit throughout the reigns of Henry, Edward, and Mary, and into the reign of Elizabeth. He died on August 29, 1559.

Elizabeth took this occasion to divide the office into three, the Revels, the Tents, and the Toyles; and the Mastership of the Revels she bestowed upon Sir Thomas Benger, by a patent dated January 18, 1560.[2] Benger died in 1572,[3] and for a time the management of the

---

[1] Cawarden was appointed on March 16, 1544; the patent is dated March 11, 1545. The patent is printed in full in Rymer, *Fœdera*, xv, 62–63; Feuillerat, *Documents*, p. 53; Halliwell-Phillipps, *Collection*, p. 1. Chalmers writes in his *Apology*, p. 494: "Sir George Bucke describes the arms of the office of the Revels as follows; though no grant of them by the College of Arms can now be found:—'Gules, a cross argent; and in the first corner of the scutcheon a Mercuries *petasus* argent; and a lyon gules in chief or'."

[2] The patent is printed by Rymer, *Fœdera*, xv. 565; Feuillerat, *Documents*, p. 54; and, from a different source, by Collier, *History of English Dramatic Poetry* (1879), i. 170.

[3] Not, as is commonly stated, in 1577; see Feuillerat, *Documents*, p. 428.

Office was placed in the hands of the clerk, Thomas Blagrove. In December, 1578, however, the Queen appointed Edmund Tilney to the vacant position.[1]

Tilney seems to have possessed extraordinary business ability, and an unusual amount of energy. Not only did he control with a firm hand all the entertainments at Court, but he gradually extended his authority over plays and professional actors throughout London and the kingdom at large. In 1581 he secured from the Queen a formal "Commission Touching the Powers of the Master," two clauses of which seem to have constituted the main authority on which he and his successors exercised jurisdiction over the public drama. So important are these clauses, and so generally neglected by students of the Revels, that I quote them in full:

And furthermore also we have and do by these presents authorize and command our said servant, Edmunde Tilney, Master of our said Revels, by himself, or his sufficient deputy or deputies, to warn, command, and appoint in all places within this our realm of England, as well within franchises and liberties as without, all and every player or players, with their playmakers, either belonging to any nobleman, or otherwise, bearing the name or names of using the faculty of playmakers, or players of comedies, tragedies, interludes, or what other showes soever, from time to time, and at all times, to appear before him with all such plays, tragedies, comedies, or shows, as they shall have in readiness, or mean to set forth, and them to present and recite before our said servant, or his sufficient deputy, whom we ordain, appoint, and authorise by these presents, of all such shows, plays, players, and playmakers, together with their playing places, to order and reform, authorise and put down, as shall be thought meet or unmeet unto himself, or his said deputy in that behalf.

And also likewise we have by these presents authorized and commanded the said Edmunde Tilney that in case if any of them, whatsoever they be, will obstinately refuse upon warning unto them given by the said Edmunde, or his sufficient deputy,

[1] The patent, which was not issued until July 24, 1579, is printed in Feuillerat, *Documents*, p. 55, and in Halliwell-Phillipps, *Collection*, p. 2.

to accomplish and obey our commandment in this behalf, then it shall be lawful to the said Edmunde, or his sufficient deputy, to attach the party or parties so offending, and him or them to commit to ward, to remain without bail or mainprise until such time as the same Edmunde Tilney, or his sufficient deputy, shall think the time of his or their imprisonment to be punishment sufficient for his or their said offences in that behalf; and that done, to enlarge him or them so being imprisoned at their plain liberty, without any loss, penalty, forfeiture, or other danger in this behalf to be sustained or borne by the said Edmunde Tilney, or his deputy, any act, statute, ordinance, or provision heretofore had or made to the contrary hereof in any wise notwithstanding.[1]

By virtue of this commission Tilney assumed the right to license all plays intended for performance before the public; we find him informing "all Justices, Mayors, Sheriffs, Bailiffs, Constables, and other" officers, that "no play is to be played but such as is allowed by the said Edmunde, and by his hand at the latter end of the said book they do play."[2] He assumed also the right to license companies of actors, and to grant them permission to travel in the country. Finally, he assumed the right to license the erection of playhouses, and to charge a regular annual fee for their "allowance."[3]

In spite of his royal commission, however, Tilney was not able to extend his authority beyond the limits of the Court without difficulty; and for many years his jurisdiction over "plays, players, and playhouses" was far from complete. The Privy Council often interfered in dramatic affairs without consulting or even so much as notifying the Master of the Revels; the Lord Chamberlain sometimes licensed plays without referring them to his subordinate; and the Common Council of London

---

[1] The commission is printed in Feuillerat, *Documents*, p. 51. It was reissued to Buc in 1603, and to Astley in 1622.

[2] See William Kelly, *Notices Illustrative of the Drama*, pp. 211–212.

[3] We find Henslowe paying him an annual fee of £2 before the year 1598 and £3 after 1599.

long asserted its inherent right to control exhibitions within the city. But Tilney's power grew with the years, until by the end of the century he had succeeded in having his jurisdiction over the public drama fully recognized. In 1660, Herbert, then Master of the Revels, was able to declare that "plays, players, and playmakers, and the permission for erecting of playhouses, have been allowed, ordered, and permitted by the Masters of His Majesty's Office of the Revels, my predecessors, successively, time out of mind, whereof the memory of man is not to the contrary."

In 1597 the reversion of the Mastership was secured by Tilney for his nephew, Sir George Buc,[1] who thereafter served as deputy. After the year 1607 Buc apparently performed all the duties of the office; and when Tilney died, August 20, 1610, he became by virtue of the grant of the reversion automatically the Master of the Revels.

On April 3, 1612, King James granted the reversion of the office to Sir John Astley; and on October 5, 1621, he granted a second reversion to Ben Jonson, to become effective at the death of Astley. A few months later there appeared at Court still a third aspirant to the office, Henry Herbert, the younger brother of George Herbert, the poet, and of Edward Herbert, Lord of Cherbury, and the near kinsman of William Herbert, Earl of Pembroke, who as Lord Chamberlain had general supervision of the Revels Office. Of his introduction to the Court Henry Herbert writes:

I was sworen King James his servant, by Sir George Keene, in ordinary gentleman of his privy chamber, the 20th March, 1621[2], at Whitehall.[2]

---

[1] To the great distress of John Lyly; see R. W. Bond, *The Complete Works of John Lyly*, 1902, i. 33; 64–65; 70–71. The reversion to Buc was confirmed by King James in 1603.

[2] Rebecca Warner, *Epistolary Curiosities*, p. 3; cf. Chalmers, *Apology*, p. 615. The position was reaffirmed at the Restoration; see his "Warrant to be Gentleman of the Privy Chamber," Egerton MS. 2542, f. 361.

No doubt his powerful relations at Court stood ready to advance him still further when opportunity offered.

Very shortly after, in May, 1622, Sir George Buc, having become weak of mind, was formally judged incapable of performing the duties of the office,[1] and Sir John Astley, by virtue of his reversion, succeeded to the Mastership.[2] For a time Astley performed the duties of the position; but on July 20, 1623, he was induced to sell the office to young Henry Herbert for the sum of £150 a year.[3]

That the Lord Chamberlain exercised his influence in securing the office for his kinsman is highly likely. We know that a month later, while entertaining the king at Wilton, the ancient family seat of the Herberts, he took occasion to introduce the new Master to royal favor. Sir Henry narrates the episode as follows:

Itt pleased the King, att my Lord Chamberline's motion, to sende for mee unto his chamber, by James Palmer, and to knighte mee, with my Lord Marquis Hamilton's sworde. He was pleased likewise to bestowe many good wordes upon mee, and to receive mee as Master of the Revells. At Wilton, this 7th August, 1623.

I sente the certificate of my knitehood, under my Lord Chamberline's hande, to the Earl Marshall, whereupon he certified to the office of the Harolds, and 'twas entered in their booke the 14th of August, 1623. The Harolds had no fee, but the Lord Marshal's Secretarys 10s.[4]

[1] He died on September 20, 1623. The date usually given, September 22, is an error; see p. 67.

[2] A commission to this effect was issued to him on May 22, 1622; see W. C. Hazlitt, *The English Drama and Stage*, p. 52, and *State Papers, Domestic Series, 1619–1623*, p. 386.

[3] See Peter Cunningham, *Extracts from the Accounts of the Revels*, p. xlix, and Chalmers, *Apology*, p. 495, note. That Herbert took charge of the office immediately after his purchase is indicated by a change in the form of the license entries. Astley, of course, remained technically the Master until his death in 1641, even though the King and the Court received Herbert as the Master in fact. In 1629 Herbert and Simon Thelwall received a reversionary grant of the office.

[4] Rebecca Warner, *Epistolary Curiosities*, p. 3; cf. Chalmers, *Apology*, p. 615, and Malone, *Variorum*, iii. 58.

Herbert thus auspiciously entered upon his long career as dictator in the dramatic world, "a place which," wrote Isaak Walton, "required a diligent wisdom, with which God hath blessed him." [1] He was blessed also with worldly wisdom. His brother Edward, Lord Herbert of Cherbury, informs us that "he attained to a great fortune," and became "dexterous in the ways of the Court, as having gotten much by it." [2] In 1627 he was able to buy for £3,000 an ancient moated house, Ribbesford, near Bewdley in Worcestershire, which he made into a fine county residence for himself and his descendants.

As Master of the Revels, Herbert experienced no serious difficulties until 1642. At the outbreak of the Civil War, however, his duties in connection with the drama came to an end; he promptly closed the Office and took the field in behalf of his king. After the Restoration he struggled hard to re-establish the Office in its former powers; but the times had changed, and he never fully succeeded. He died on April 27, 1673. [3]

## II. THE HERBERT MANUSCRIPTS

It was customary for each Master of the Revels to keep an office-book in which he recorded, as in a diary, the business transacted by himself or his deputy. The books thus kept by Tilney and Buc were accessible to

---

[1] Isaak Walton, *The Life of Mr. George Herbert.*
[2] *The Autobiography of Edward Lord Herbert of Cherbury* (ed. Sidney L. Lee, p. 22).
[3] For the life of Herbert see, in addition to the documents printed in this volume, *Collections Historical and Archæological Relating to Montgomeryshire and Its Borders*, issued by the Powys-Land Club, vii. 150 ff., xi. 346 ff.; Rebecca Warner, *Epistolary Curiosities;* and the article by Sir Sidney Lee in *The Dictionary of National Biography.*

Herbert, who quotes from them frequently;[1] since then, however, they have disappeared, and the only vestiges of them now preserved are Herbert's quotations.[2] When Herbert purchased the Mastership from Sir John Astley in 1623, he merely continued the office-book which Astley had already begun.[3] And this book, extending from 1622 to 1642, with other important manuscripts, he left at his death in a certain chest in his library at Ribbesford. His only son, created Lord Herbert of Cherbury, died in 1709, and left Ribbesford to his only son, the second Lord Herbert of Cherbury. The second Lord Herbert of Cherbury, dying childless in 1738, left the estate to a cousin, Henry Morley; Morley, dying in 1781, left it to his sister, Magdalena, who, dying in the following year, left it to her kinsman, George Paulet, Marquis of Winchester; finally, Winchester, in 1787, sold it to Francis Ingram, Esq., of Ticknell. Chalmers writes in his *Apology*, p. 525:

In consequence of all those family failures, there remained at Ribbesford nothing of the Herbert's but the *Old Chest*, which contained the life of the famous Lord Herbert of Cherbery, that was published by the Earl of Oxford; and the office-book of Sir Henry, containing many scenic particulars that were given to the world by Mr. Malone, being enabled to gratify curiosity by the liberal communication of Mr. Francis Ingram of Ribbesford.

And Malone writes (*Var*. iii. 59):

The office-book of Sir Henry Herbert contains an account of almost every piece exhibited at any of the theatres from August 1623, to the commencement of the rebellion in 1641, and many curious anecdotes relative to them, some of which I shall presently have occasion to quote.

---

[1] Apparently even so late as 1662; see p. 112. It is generally stated, but on insufficient grounds (see *S. A.*, p. 203), that Buc's office-book was destroyed by fire before 1624.

[2] See pp. 18, 22, 25, 26, 28, 35, 42, 48, 49, 105, 112.

[3] See pp. 48, 49. Herbert makes his entry of licenses in a form slightly different from Astley's.

Again he says (*Var*. iii. 57):

For the use of this very curious and valuable manuscript I am indebted to Francis Ingram, of Ribbisford near Bewdley in Worcestershire, Esq. Deputy Remembrancer in the Court of Exchequer. It has lately been found in the same old chest which contained the manuscript *Memoirs of Lord Herbert of Cherbury*, from which Mr. Walpole about twenty years ago printed the Life of that nobleman, who was elder brother to Sir Henry Herbert.

Both Malone and Chalmers were allowed to examine the office-book and to make liberal extracts therefrom. Since then, however, the manuscript has disappeared. Possibly it has perished, for Malone as early as 1790 speaks of it as being in a decayed condition (*Var*. iii. 59):

This valuable manuscript having lain for a considerable time in a damp place, is unfortunately damaged, and in a very mouldering condition.

In the present volume I have attempted to bring together all the quotations made by Malone and Chalmers from the Office-Book, and also all the statements which they profess to base on their study of that document.[1]

But the office-book was not the only manuscript of dramatic importance preserved by Herbert; many of the records of his connection with the Revels after the Restoration were also kept by him, largely as a result of his lawsuits with Davenant and with Killigrew's actors, and his attempts to re-establish the ancient authority of the Office. It was not originally my

---

[1] Malone printed extracts in his essay on *Shakspeare, Ford, and Jonson* (see *Var*. i. 402 ff.), and in his *Historical Account of the English Stage* (see *Var*. iii). Chalmers first secured independent extracts from the office-book after he had written his *Apology*, but in an Appendix, p. 615, he adds a few notes therefrom which "came to hand after the foregoing sheets were printed"; in his *Supplemental Apology* he quotes freely from the office-book. In Malone's *Inquiry into the Authenticity*, etc., 1796, I find one statement based on the "Herbert MS."

purpose to include these documents; but after I had
gathered them I found that they illustrated so many
things in the office-book, and furnished so much material valuable for the later history of the Revels Office
and for the history of the Restoration drama, that I
decided to append them, though without annotation.

Some of the documents were reproduced by Ma-
lone in his *History of the Stage*, especially those relating
to Herbert's difficulties with Davenant and Killigrew.
Nearly all of these, with many others, were printed by
Halliwell-Phillipps in a privately issued volume (limited
to eleven copies) entitled *A Collection of Ancient Documents Respecting the Office of the Master of the Revels*,
1870. The documents were most carefully reproduced,
virtually in type-facsimile, "from the original manuscripts formerly in the Haslewood Collection." This
collection is now preserved in the British Museum in a
large quarto volume (Addit. MS. 19,256). Because of
the present war-conditions in Europe, and especially
the danger of entrusting manuscript to the high seas,
I have contented myself with reproducing Halliwell-
Phillipps's painstaking reprint of the documents.[1] Possibly a collation of the reprint with the originals would
reveal some errors in punctuation or spelling; but for
the purposes of this book such errors are unimportant.[2]

In 1818, Mrs. Rebecca Thayer had access to an

[1] In preparing his cases at law against Davenant and Betterton, Herbert
had copies made of various early documents relating to the Revels. I have
not reproduced these when they are available elsewhere in more accurate form.
The omitted documents are listed below: patents to Cawarden, Tilney, and
Buc as Masters of the Revels; patent to Kirkham as Yeoman of the Revels;
two patents to Huninge as Clerk Comptroller; a history of the Revels Office,
written in 1573 (the original is printed by Feuillerat, *Documents*). All these
documents relate to the period before Herbert became Master. Of the
documents after Herbert became Master I have omitted three: a private
letter from Beatrice Herbert, his niece, dated December 13, 1653; a patent
to Henry Harris as Yeoman of the Revels; a patent to Alexander Stafford as
Clerk Comptroller of the Revels.

[2] I have collated all the documents reproduced by both Malone and
Halliwell-Phillipps, and recorded in footnotes the significant variations.

entirely different collection of Herbert documents,[1] the more interesting of which she printed in her *Epistolary Curiosities*. I have not been able to discover what has become of this collection; in 1905, however, two or three of the manuscripts found their way into the British Museum (Addit. MS. 37,157). I have reprinted from the *Epistolary Curiosities* all the documents which relate in any way to the Revels Office or to the drama.[2]

[1] Is it possible that she had the office-book itself in her possession? The passage which Chalmers, *Apology*, p. 615, quotes as from the office-book she quotes, p. 2, as "from MSS. in the editor's hands." Chalmers, however, may have been mistaken, for at that time he had not personally examined the Herbert papers.

[2] In the Public Record Office, London (Audit Office Accounts, Various, Bundle 1214) are preserved the official account books of the Revels Office from 1660 to 1670; but in these formal accounts plays are mentioned only incidentally, if at all. The present war in Europe has made it impossible for me to examine these records.

# THE OFFICE BOOK, 1622–1642

# THE OFFICE-BOOK, 1622–1642

## I. CENSORSHIP OF PLAYS

Edmund Tilney, as we have seen, first established
the right of the Master of the Revels to censor plays
and license them for public representation; "no play
is to be played but such as is allowed," he announced,
and the evidence of such allowance was to be a formal
notice to that effect written and signed by the Master
"at the latter end of the said book they do play."
Edward Hayward writes:[1]

That the Master of his Majesties office of the Revells, hath
the power of Lycencing all playes, whether Tragedies, or Comedies, before they can bee acted, is without dispute; and the
designe is that all prophaneness, oathes, ribaldry, and matters
reflecting upon piety, and the present government may bee
obliterated before there bee any action in a publique Theatre.

The fee charged by the Master for licensing a play
varied much from the time of Elizabeth to the outbreak of the Civil War.[2]   From Henslowe's *Diary* we
learn that Tilney charged 7s. a play.[3]   Buc seems to
have charged £1; and this was at first the regular
charge made by Herbert.   When, however, the correcting of a play entailed unusual labor, demanding, probably, a second reading, Herbert charged £2; and after
about the year 1632 he regularly charged £2 for licensing a new play, and £1 for allowing an old play to be

[1] See page 125.
[2] See p. 119.
[3] See Greg, *Henslowe's Diary*, ii. 113–116.

revived.[1]  His charges for minor alterations and for additions to plays varied.from 10s. to £1.[2]

For an example of the censorship as practised by Tilney one may examine the manuscript of *Sir Thomas More*,[3] and for examples of Buc's censorship, the manuscripts of *The Second Maiden's Tragedy*[4] and *Sir John van Olden Barnavelt*.[5]  To illustrate Herbert's censorship I have brought together all the passages from his office-book which bear on the subject.[6]

**1623, August.**  "For the Company at the Curtain; A Tragedy of *the Plantation of Virginia; the profaneness to be left out*, otherwise not tolerated."  (*S. A. 214*.)

**1623, August 19.**  "For the king's players.  An olde playe called *Winter's Tale*, formerly allowed of by Sir George Bucke, and likewyse by mee on Mr. Hemmings his worde that there was nothing profane added or reformed, thogh the allowed booke was missinge;[1] and therefore I returned it without a fee, this 19 of August, 1623."  (*Var. iii. 229*.)

**1623-4, January 2.**  "For the Palsgrave's Company; *The History of the Dutchess of Suffolk;* which being full of dangerous matter was much reformed by me; I had two pounds for my pains: Written by Mr. Drew."  (*S. A. 217*.)

**1624-5, January 25.**  "For the Prince's Company; A new Play, called, *The Widow's Prize;* which containing much abusive

---

[1] In 1662 Herbert stated in a letter to the Lord High Chancellor that before the Civil War his customary fee for licensing had been: "For a new play, to bee brought with the booke, £2.  For an old play, to be brought with the booke, £1."  And he succeeded shortly after in having this schedule of fees re-established for the Restoration.  See pp. 84, 121, 138.

[2] See pp. 29, 32, 37.

[3] The manuscript (MS. Harley 7368) has been photographically reproduced in *The Tudor Facsimile Texts;* it may also be studied to advantage in the Malone Society's reprint.

[4] The manuscript (Lansdowne MS. 807) has been photographically reproduced in *The Tudor Facsimile Texts*.

[5] The play (British Museum Addit. MS. 18,653) has been reprinted by Mr. A. H. Bullen in *Old English Plays*, vol. ii.

[6] For a general discussion of censorship one should consult Virginia C. Gildersleeve, *Government Regulation of the Elizabethan Drama*, 1908; Frank Fowell and Frank Palmer, *Censorship in England*, 1913; and G. M. G., *The Stage Censor, 1544-1907*, 1908.

[7] Possibly burned with the Globe.

matter, was allowed of by me, on condition, that my reformations were observed."[1]  (*S. A.* 219–220.)

**1630–1, January 11.** "This day being the 11 of Janu 1630 I did refuse to allow of a play of Messinger's because itt did contain dangerous matter, as the deposing of Sebastian king of Portugal, by Philip the [Second,] and ther being a peace sworen twixte the kings of England and Spayne.[2]  I had my fee not withstandinge, which belongs to me for reading itt over, and ought to be brought always with the booke."  (*Var.* iii. 229–231.)

**1632, November 18.** "18 Nov. 1632. In the play of *The Ball,* written by Sherley, and acted by the Queens players,[3] ther were divers personated so naturally, both of lords and others of the court, that I took it ill, and would have forbidden the play, but that Biston [Christopher Beeston, the manager] promiste many things which I found faulte withall should be left out,[4] and that he would not suffer it to be done by the poett any more, who deserves to be punisht; and the first that offends in this kind, of poets or players, shall be sure of publique punishment." (*Var.* iii. 231–232.)

**1633, May 7.** "R. for allowinge of *The Tale of the Tubb,* Vitru Hoop's parte wholly strucke out, and the motion of the tubb, by commande from my lorde chamberlin; exceptions being taken against it by Inigo Jones, surveyor of the kings workes, as a personal injury unto him. May 7, 1633,—2*l*. 0. 0." (*Var.* iii. 232.)

**1633, July 3.** "The comedy called *The Yonge Admirall,* being free from oaths, prophaness, or obsceanes, hath given mee much delight and satisfaction in the readinge, and may serve for a patterne to other poetts, not only for the bettring of maners and language, but for the improvement of the quality, which hath received some brushings of late.

"When Mr. Sherley hath read this approbation, I know it will encourage him to pursue this beneficiall and cleanly way of poetry, and when other poetts heare and see his good successe. I am confident they will imitate the original for their own credit, and make such copies in this harmless way, as shall speak them

---

[1] Fleay, *B. C. E. D.* ii. 175, doubted the existence of this entry, which he could not find "in S. R., Malone, or Chalmers."
[2] This play has been identified as Massinger's *Believe as Ye List,* formerly licensed by Herbert on May 7, 1631.  See p. 33, note 4.
[3] Herbert licensed the play on November 16, 1632.
[4] For a discussion of the revision see Fleay, *B. C. E. D.* ii. 239.

masters in their art, at the first sight, to all judicious spectators. It may be acted this 3 July, 1633.

"I have entered this allowance, for direction to my successor, and for example to all poetts, that shall write after the date hereof." (*Var.* iii. 232–233.)

**1633, October.** "Octob, 1633. Exception was taken by Mr. Sewster to the second part of *The Citty Shuffler*,¹ which gave me occasion to stay the play, till the company [of Salisbury Court] had given him satisfaction; which was done the next day, and under his hande he did certifye mee that he was satisfyed." *MS. Herbert.* (*Var.* iii. 172.)

**1633, October 18.** "On friday the nineteenth [an error for "eighteenth"] of October, 1633, I sent a warrant by a messenger of the chamber to suppress *The Tamer Tamd*,² to the Kings players, for that afternoone, and it was obeyd; upon complaints of foule and offensive matters conteyned therein.

"They acted *The Scornful Lady* instead of it, I have enterd the warrant here:

" 'These are to will and require you to forbeare the actinge of your play called *The Tamer Tamd, or the Taminge of the Tamer*, this afternoone, or any more till you have leave from mee: and this at your perill.   On friday morninge the 18 Octob. 1633.

" 'To Mr. Taylor, Mr. Lowins, or any of the King's players at the Blackfryers.'

"On saterday morninge followinge the booke was brought mee, and at my lord of Hollands request I returned it to the players ye monday morninge after, purgd of oaths, prophaness, and ribaldrye, being yᵉ 21 of Octob. 1633.

"Because the stoppinge of the acting of this play for that afternoone, it being an ould play, hath raysed some discourse in the players, thogh no disobedience, I have thought fitt to insert here ther submission upon a former disobedience, and to declare that it concernes the Master of the Revells to bee carefull of their ould revived playes, as of their new, since they may conteyne offensive matter, which ought not to be allowed in any time.

"The Master ought to have copies of their new playes left with him, that he may be able to shew what he hath allowed or disallowed.

---

¹ This play is not extant.   The title appears in Warburton's list.
² *The Woman's Prize*, by Fletcher.   It was performed at Court on November 28, 1633   and "very well likt"; see p. 53.

"All ould plays ought to bee brought to the Master of the Revells, and have his allowance to them, for which he should have his fee, since they may be full of offensive things against church and state; y⁰ rather that in former time the poetts tooke greater liberty than is allowed them by mee.

"The players ought not to study their parts till I have allowed of the booke.

"'To Sir Henry Herbert, Kᵗ. master of his Ma.ᵗⁱᵉᵐ Revels.'

"'After our humble servise remembered unto your good wor ship, Whereas not long since we acted a play called *The Spanishe Viceroy*, not being licensed under your worships hande, nor allowd of: wee doe confess and herby acknowledge that wee have offended, and that it is in your power to punishe this offense, and are very sorry for it; and doe likewise promise herby that wee will not act any play without your hand or substituts hereafter, nor doe any thinge that may prejudice the authority of your office: So hoping that this humble submission of ours may bee accepted, wee have therunto sett our hands. This twentiethe of Decemb. 1624.

| | |
|---|---|
| Joseph Taylor. | John Lowen. |
| Richard Robinson. | John Shancke. |
| Elyard Swanston. | John Rice. |
| Thomas Pollard. | Will. Rowley. |
| Robert Benfeilde. | Richard Sharpe.' |
| George Burght. | |

"'Mr. Knight,

"'In many things you have saved mee labour; yet wher your judgment or penn fayld you, I have made boulde to use mine. Purge ther parts, as I have the booke. And I hope every hearer and player will thinke that I have done God good servise, and the quality no wronge; who hath no greater enemies than oaths, prophaness, and publique ribaldry, whᶜʰ for the future I doe absolutely forbid to bee presented unto mee in any playbooke, as you will answer it at your perill. 21 Octob. 1633.'

"This was subscribed to their play of *The Tamer Tamd*, and directed to Knight, their book-keeper.

"The 24 Octob. 1633, Lowins and Swanston were sorry for their ill manners, and craved my pardon, which I gave them in presence of Mr. Taylor and Mr. Benfeilde." (*Var.* iii. 208 210.)

**1633, October 24.** "Upon a second petition of the players to the High Commission court, wherein they did mee right in my

¹ In the margin here Sir Henry Herbert has added this note: "'Tis entered here for a rememberance against their disorders."

care to purge their plays of all offense, my lords Grace of Canter-
bury bestowed many words upon mee, and discharged mee of
any blame, and layd the whole fault of their play, called *The
Magnetick Lady*,[1] upon the players. This happened the 24 of
Octob. 1633, at Lambeth. In their first petition they would
have excused themselves on mee and the poett." (*Var.* iii. 233.)

**1633, November 23.** "The Kings players sent me an ould
booke of Fletchers called *The Loyal Subject*, formerly allowed by
Sir George Bucke, 16 Novemb. 1618, which according to their
desire and agreement I did peruse, and with some reformations
allowed of, the 23 of Nov. 1633, for which they sent mee according
to their promise 1*l.* o. o." (*Var.* iii. 234.)

**1633-4, January 9.** "This morning, being the 9th of January,
1633, the kinge was pleasd to call mee into his withdrawinge
chamber to the windowe, wher he went over all that I had croste
in Davenants play-booke,[2] and allowing of *faith* and *slight* to
bee asseverations only, and no oathes, markt them to stande,
and some other few things, but in the greater part allowed of
my reformations. This was done upon a complaint of Mr.
Endymion Porters in December.

"The kinge is pleasd to take *faith, death, slight*, for asseverations, and no oaths, to which I doe humbly submit as my masters
judgment; but, under favour, conceive them to be oaths, and
enter them here, to declare my opinion and submission.

"The 10 of January, 1633, I returned unto Mr. Davenant his
playe-booke of *The Witts*, corrected by the kinge.

"The kinge would not take the booke at Mr. Porters hands;
but commanded him to bring it unto mee, which he did, and
likewise commanded Davenant to come to me for it, as I believe:
otherwise he would not have byn so civill." (*Var.* iii. 235.)

**1638, June 5.** "Received of Mr. Lowens for my paines about
Messinger's play called *The King and the Subject*, 2 June, 1638,
1*l.* o. o.

"The name of *The King and the Subject* is altered,[3] and I
allowed the play to bee acted, the reformations most strictly
observed, and not otherwise, the 5th of June, 1638.

"At Greenwich the 4 of June, Mr. W. Murray, gave mee
power from the king to allowe of the play, and tould me that
hee would warrant it.

[1] Herbert licensed this play on October 12, 1632.
[2] *The Witts.* For its success on the public stage and at Court see p. 54.
[3] Possibly altered to *The Tyrant*, a play which was entered on the Stationers' Registers, June 29, 1660, but not printed; see page 38, note 2.

"'Monys? Wee'le rayse supplies what ways we please,
"'And force you to subscribe to blanks, in which
"'We'le mulct you as wee shall thinke fitt. The Caesars
"'In Rome were wise, acknowledginge no lawes
"'But what their swords did ratifye, the wives
"'And daughters of the senators bowinge to
"'Their wills, as deities,' &c.

"This is a peece taken out of Phillip Messingers play, called *The King and the Subject*, and entered here for ever to bee remembered by my son and those that cast their eyes on it, in honour of Kinge Charles, my master, who readinge over the play at Newmarket, set his marke upon the place with his owne hande, and in thes words:

"'This is too insolent, and to bee changed.'

"Note, that the poett makes it the speech of a king, Don Pedro, king of Spayne, and spoken to his subjects." (*Var.* iii. 240.)

**1642, June.** "[1642. June.] Received of Mr. Kirke, for a new play which I burnte for the ribaldry and offense that was in it, 2*l.* 0. 0." (*Var.* iii. 241.)

## II. LICENSES OF PLAYS

**1622, May 10.** "A new Play, called, *The Blacke Ladye*, was allowed to be acted by the Lady Elizabeth's Servants." [1] (*S. A.* 213.)

**1622, May 10.** "A new Play, called, *The Welsh Traveller*,[2] was allowed to be acted by the players of the Revels." (*S. A.* 213.)

**1622, May 14.** A new play called *The Prophetess*, licensed May 14, 1622. (*Var.* iii. 226.)

[1] The play is not extant. Chalmers gives the date for this entry and the three entries following it (May 10, June 3, June 10) as 1622; Fleay, *History of the Stage*, p. 301, and subsequent scholars have altered this to 1623, possibly rightly, for the children of the Revels, mentioned in the second entry, were not granted their patent until July 8, 1622.

[2] Possibly the same as *The Welsh Ambassador*, a play existing in a manuscript in private hands, which has been sometimes misquoted under the title *The Witch Traveller*. See W. C. Hazlitt, *A Manual for the Collector and Amateur of Old English Plays*, p. 250. On the date, see the preceding footnote.

**1622, June 3.** "A new Play, called, *The Valiant Scholler*,[1] allowed to be acted by the Lady Elizabeth's Servants." (*S. A.* 213.)

**1622, June 10.** "A new Play, called, *The Duche Painter, and the French Branke*,[2] was allowed to be acted by the Princes Servants at the Curtayne." (*S. A.* 213.)

**1622, June 22.** *The Sea Voyage.* This piece was acted at the Globe. (*Var.* iii. 226.)

**1622, October 24.** *The Spanish Curate.* Acted at Black-friars. (*Var.* iii. 226.)

**?1623, May 10.** [See note under 1622, May 10.]

**?1623, June 3.** [See note under 1622, May 10.]

**?1623, June 10.** [See note under 1622, May 10.]

**1623, July 27.** "For the Palsgrave's Players, a Tragedy of *Richard the Third, or the English Profit*,[3] with the Reformation, written by Samuel Rowley." (*S. A.* 214.)

**1623, July 30.** "For the Prince's Players, A French Tragedy of *the Bellman of Paris*,[4] written by Thomas Dekkirs and John Day, for the Company of the Red Bull." (*S. A.* 214.)

**1623, August.** "For the Company at the Curtain; A Tragedy of *the Plantation of Virginia*;[5] the profaneness to be left out, otherwise not tolerated." (*S. A.* 214.)

**1623, August 19.** "For the Prince's Servants of the Red Bull; an Oulde Playe, called, *The Peaceable King; or the Lord*

---

[1] Not extant. On the date see the note to the entry 1622, May 10.

[2] Not extant. Fleay, *B. C. E. D.* ii. 156, suggests that it dealt with the same story we find in *The Wisdom of Doctor Dodypol*, and adds: "*The Painter, or The Wandering Lovers*, S. R. 9th Sept. 1653, entered as Massinger's, seems more likely to have been *The Dutch Painter, or The French Branke* [Query Brinch or pledge-drink; cf. ii. 1], which was licensed 10th June 1623 for the Prince's men, than *The Wandering Lovers* (or *Lovers' Progress*), licensed for the King's men the 6th Dec. 1623." On a possible error in the date of the license see the note to the entry 1622, May 10.

[3] Not extant. Fleay, *History of the Stage*, p. 301, says that Rowley reformed or altered an old play; in *B. C. E. D.* ii. 171, he says: "This may have been only an alteration of Jonson's *Richard Crookback* of 1602." The word "reformation," however, may have been used by Herbert with reference to the censored portions.

[4] Not extant.

[5] Not extant.

*Mendall,*[1] which was formerly allowed by Sir George Bucke, and likewise by me." (*S. A.* 214.)

**1623, August 19.** "For the king's players. An olde playe called *Winter's Tale,* formerly allowed of by Sir George Bucke, and likewyse by mee on Mr. Hemmings his worde that there was nothing profane added or reformed, thogh the allowed booke was missinge;[2] and therefore I returned it without a fee, this 19 of August, 1623." (*Var.* iii. 229.)

**1623, August 21.** "For the Lady Elizabeth's Servants of the Cockpit; An Old Play, called, *Match me in London,*[3] which had been formerly allowed by Sir George Bucke." (*S. A.* 214.)

**1623, August 29.** "For the King's Players; a new Comedy, called, *The Maid of the Mill;* written by Fletcher, and Rowley." (*S. A.* 214–215; *Var.* iii. 226.)

**1623, September 12.** "For the Lady Elizabeth's Players; a new Comedy, called, *The Cra . . . Marchant, or Come to my Country house;* Written by William Bonen.[4] It was acted at the Red Bull, and licensed without my hand to itt; because they were none of the *four* Companys."[5] (*S. A.* 215.)

**1623, September 18.** "For a Company of Strangers; a new Comedy, called, *Come see a Wonder;* Written by John Deye."[6] (*S. A.* 215.)

[1] Not extant. It will be observed that the Prince's Servants are no longer spoken of as being at the Curtain, and so far as we know that ancient playhouse was not again used for dramatic purposes. Malone, presumably basing his statement on the records in Herbert's office-book, says (*Var.* iii. 54, note 2) that shortly after the accession of King Charles the First, the Curtain "seems to have been used only by prize-fighters." The building was still standing in 1627; see Jeaffreson, *Middlesex County Records,* iii. 164.

[2] Probably the "allowed booke" (i. e. the copy with the license at the end) was destroyed by the fire at the Globe in 1613. Since, however, the play was first printed in the Folio of 1623, possibly the "allowed booke" was misplaced by the printer of that volume. For a notice of a performance of the play at Court shortly after, see under 1623-4, January 18.

[3] By Thomas Dekker, written about 1611, printed in 1631.

[4] In Warburton's list we find "The Crafty Mercha[n]t C[omedy] Shack. Marmion"; in S. R., September 9, 1653, was entered "The Crafty Merchant, or The Soldered Citizen," as by Marmion; and again in S. R., September 29, 1660, was entered "The Sodered Citizen," comedy, by Marmion. The play, however, is not extant. Of Bonen little is known; his name appears again in Herbert's office-book under the date 1623, November 19.

[5] As to "the *four* Companys" see page 62. Miss Gildersleeve, in her *Government Regulation of the Elizabethan Drama,* p. 77, says: "Who else could have licensed the play is not apparent,—the Lord Chamberlain, possibly." The entry, I think, means that Herbert licensed the play, but refused to place his signature thereon, for the reason he assigns. See the next note

[6] Probably Day's *Wonder of a Kingdom.* Although I have reproduced Chalmers's transcript of this and the preceding entry, I believe that the last

1623, October 2. "For the Prince's Companye; a new Comedy, called, *A Fault in Friendship*:[1] Written by *Young* Johnson, and Broome." (These were the *Son*, and Servant, of Ben Jonson.) (*S. A.* 215.)

1623, October 17. "For the King's Company. An Old Play, called, *More Dissemblers besides Women*:[2] allowed by Sir George Bucke; and being free from alterations was allowed by me, for a new play, called, *The Devil of Dowgate, or Usury put to use*:[3] Written by Fletcher." (*S. A.* 215–216.)

1623, October 29. "For the Palsgrave's Players; a new Comedy, called, *Hardshifte for Husbands, or Bilboes the best blade*,[4] Written by Samuel Rowley." (*S. A.* 216.)

1623, November 19. "For the Palsgrave's Players; a new Tragedy, called, *Two Kings in a Cottage*; Written by Bonen." [5] (*S. A.* 216.)

1623, November 28. "For a Strange Company at the Red Bull;[6] *The Faiyre fowle one, or The bayting of the Jealous Knight*: Written by Smith." [7] (*S. A.* 216.)

1623, December 3. "For the Queen of Bohemia's Company; *The Noble Bondman*: Written by Philip Messenger, gent."— This was allowed to be printed on the 12th March 1624.[8] (*S. A.* 216; *Var.* iii. 230.)

1623, December 4. "For the Palsgrave's Players; *The Hungarian Lion*: Written by Gunnel." [9] (*S. A.* 216.)

sentence of the entry of September 12 belongs to the entry of September 18 (cf. the entry of November 28, 1623, on page 26). This is supported by Malone, who says, *Var.* iii. 224: "Sir Henry Herbert observes that the play called *Come See a Wonder*, 'written by John Daye for a company of strangers,' and represented Sept. 18, 1623, was 'acted at the Red Bull, and licensed without his hand to it, because they [i. e. this company of strangers] were none of the *four* companys.'" The error has led to much confusion—a confusion which has been increased by Fleay's misstatements.

[1] Not extant.
[2] By Thomas Middleton. It was presented at Court on January 6, 1623–4; see p. 51, note 8.
[3] Not extant. The entry is not clear. Malone, *Var.* iii. 226, notes that *The Devill of Dowgate or Usury Put to Use* was licensed for the King's Servants on October 17, 1623; and that, probably, is the correct interpretation of the entry. The play has been identified with *The Nightwalker, Wit at Several Weapons*, and *Buc is a Thief*; see Fleay, *B. C. E. D.* i. 197, 218.
[4] Not extant.
[5] The play is not extant. Bonen's name appears again in the license of 1623 September 12; nothing else in known of him.
[6] See page 25, note 6.
[7] Probably William Smith. The play is not extant.
[8] The play was entered in S. R. March 12, 1624, and printed shortly after.
[9] The play is not extant. Richard Gunnel was a distinguished actor, at

**1623, December 6.** "For the King's Company: *The Wandring Lovers*: Written by Mr. Fletcher."[1]  (*S. A.* 216; *Var.* iii. 226.)

**1623–4, January 2.** "For the Palsgrave's Company; *The History of the Dutchess of Suffolk;* which being full of dangerous matter was much reformed by me; I had two pounds for my pains: Written by Mr. Drew."[2]  (*S. A.* 217.)

**1623–4, January 6.** "For the Prince's Company; *The Four Sons of Amon;* being an Old Playe,[3] and *not of a legible hand.*" (*S. A.* 217.)

**1623–4, January 26.** "For the Palsgrave's Company; A Tragedy, called, *The whore in grain.*"[4]  (*S. A.* 217.)

**1623–4, March 3.** "For the Cockpit Company; *The Sun's Darling;* in the nature of a masque by Deker, and Forde." (*S. A.* 217.)

**1623–4, March 16.** "For the king's company. *Shankes Ordinary*, written by Shankes himself,[5] this 16 March, 1623,—1*l.* 0*s.* 0*d.*" MS. Herbert.  (*Var.* iii. 221; *S. A.* 179.)

**1624, April 6.** "For the Fortune; a new Comedy, called, *A Match or no Match.*[6] Written by Mr. Rowleye." (*S. A.* 217.)

**1624, April 10.** "For the king's company. *The Historye of*

this time the manager of the Palsgrave's Players at the Fortune. In 1629 he joined with Herbert's deputy, William Blagrove, in erecting the Salisbury Court Playhouse. In addition to this play he wrote *The Way to Content All Women* (see under the date 1624, April 17), and possibly *The Masque* (see under the date 1624, November 3).

[1] Malone, *Var.* iii. 226, says "This piece is lost." But Fleay identifies it confidently ("there can be no doubt") with *The Lovers' Progress*, which, in turn, he identifies with the *Cleander* licensed by Herbert on May 7, 1634: see his *B. C. E. D.* i. 219, ii. 156. On September 9, 1653, Mosely entered *The Wandering Lovers, or The Painter* in S. R. as by Philip Massinger; it is possible, however, that he was attempting to smuggle two plays through for the fee of one. The play does not appear in Warburton's list.

[2] The play was printed in 1631 as by Thomas Drue. In the S. R., September 9, 1653, was entered *The Woman's Mistake*, by T. Drue and R. Davenport. Fleay, *B. C. E. D.* i. 162, with positiveness assigns to Drue *The Bloody Banquet*, printed in 1620 as "by T. D."

[3] The play is mentioned in Henslowe's *Diary*, December 10, 1602, and is referred to in Heywood's *Apology for Actors*. For a discussion see Greg, *Henslowe's Diary*, ii. 227.

[4] Fleay identifies this with *The Whore* "new vampt," which caused the players so much trouble in 1639; see his *History of the Stage*, pp. 358–359.

[5] The well-known actor at the Globe and Blackfriars. His *Ordinary* is not extant.

[6] Not extant.

*Henry the First*, written by Damport [Davenport];[1] this 10 April, 1624,—1*l*. o. o." (*Var.* iii. 229; 319.)

**1624, April 17.** "For the Fortune; *The way to content all Women, or how a Man may please his Wife*: Written by Mr. Gunnel."[2] (*S. A.* 217.)

**1624, April 17.** "For the Cockpit; *The Renegado, or the Gentleman of Venice*:[3] Written by Messenger." (*S. A.* 218; *Var.* iii. 230.)

**1624, May 3.** "For the Prince's Company; A New Play, called, *The Madcap*: Written by *Barnes*."[4] (*S. A.* 218.)

**1624, May 3.** "An Old Play, called, *Jugurth, King of Numidia*, formerly allowed by Sir George Bucke."[5] (*S. A.* 218.)

**1624, May 15.** The Tragedy of *Nero* was allowed to be printed.[6] (*S. A.* 218.)

**1624, May 21.** "For the Palsgrave's Company; a Playe, called, *Honour in the End*."[7] (*S. A.* 218.)

**1624, May 27.** "For the King's Company, A Comedy, called, *A Wife for a Month*:[8] Written by Fletcher." (*S. A.* 218; *Var.* iii. 226.)

**1624, May 27.** "For the Prince's Company; A Play, called, *The Parracide*."[9] (*S. A.* 218.)

[1] In S. R., September 9, 1653, was entered *Henry 1 and Henry 2*, "by Shakespeare and Davenport"; and in Warburton's list we find entered: "Henry ye I^st. by Will Shakespear & Rob. Davenport." The play is not extant.

[2] The play is not extant. For what is known of the author see the note under the entry of 1623, December 4.

[3] Published in 1630 with the first title only. On October 30, 1639, Herbert licensed a play by Shirley with the title *The Gentleman of Venice*.

[4] The play is not extant. Of the author nothing is known.

[5] Elsewhere Chalmers writes (*S. A.* 203): "On the 3d of May, 1624, Sir Henry Herbert states, that he had licensed, without a fee, *Jugurth*, an old play, allowed by Sir George Bucke, and *burnt, with his other books*." In Henslowe's *Diary*, ed. Greg, p. 118, we read: "lent vnto me W birde the 9 of februarye [1600] to paye for a new booke to will: Boyle. cal'd Jugurth xxx^s w^c if yo^u dislike Ile repaye it back." Apparently this is the play now licensed by Herbert.

[6] The play was printed in 1624. A MS. of the play is preserved in the British Museum (Egerton MSS. 1994). Fleay, *B. C. E. D.* ii. 84, suggests Thomas May as the author.

[7] Not extant. In *Naps Upon Parnassus*, 1658, and *Wit and Drollery*, 1661, the play is advertised as being in the press; since, however, it does not appear in the later and more exhaustive catalogues of plays presumably it was never printed. Fleay regularly refers to it as "Humour in the End."

[8] It was acted at Court on February 9, 1636-7.

[9] *The Parracide, or Revenge for Honor* was entered S. R. November 29, 1653, as by Glapthorne, and printed in 1654 with the title *Revenge for Honor*,

**1624, June 11.** "A new play, called, *The Fairy Knight:* Written by Forde, and Decker." [1]  (*S. A.* 218.)

**1624, July 7.** "For the adding of a scene to *The Virgin Martyr*,[2] this 7th July, 1624,—£0. 10. 0." (*Var.* i. 424.)

**1624, August.** [In the Privy Council Record, August 21, 1624, we read that Middleton's *Game at Chess* had been "seen and allowed by Sir Henry Herbert, Knt., Master of the Revels, under his own hand, and subscribed in the last page of the said book." See also *Calendar of State Papers, Domestic, 1623-1625,* p. 329.]

**1624, September 3.** "For the Cockpit Company; A new Play, called, *The Captive, or The Lost recovered:* Written by Hayward." [3]  (*S. A.* 218.)

**1624, September.** "A new Tragedy, called, *A Late Murther of the Sonn upon the Mother:* Written by Forde, and Webster." [4]  (*S. A.* 218–219.)

**1624, September 15.** "For the Palsgrave's Company; A Tragedy, called, *The Faire Star of Antwerp.*" [5]  (*S. A.* 219.)

**1624, October 14.** "For the Cockpit Company; A new Play, called, *The City Night Cap:* Written by Davenport." (*S. A.* 219.)

**1624, October 15.** "For the Palsgrave's Company; A new Play, called, *The Angell King.*" [6]  (*S. A.* 219.)

**1624, October 19.** *Rule a Wife and Have a Wife,* by John Fletcher, licensed. (*Var.* iii. 226.)

as by George Chapman. Swinburne was inclined to believe Chapman the author; Fleay confesses (*B. C. E. D.* ii. 327): "There is no author known to me to whom I can assign it." Yet a comparison of the play with the known works of Glapthorne will leave no doubt whatever but that Glapthorne was the author.

[1] Presumably this play was licensed to the Prince's Company, whose name appears just above. It is not extant; Fleay writes, *B. C. E. D.* i. 232: "Query, *Huon of Bordeaux* refashioned."

[2] The play had been licensed by Sir George Buc on October 6, 1620, and published in 1622 as by Dekker and Massinger. Fleay, *B. C. E. D.* i. 213, says: "The original play was doubtless *Dioclesian,* acted at the Rose 1594, Nov. 16, but even then an old play, dating from 1591 at the latest."

[3] Thomas Heywood. The MS. is preserved in the British Museum, and has been printed by Mr. Bullen in his *Collection of Old English Plays.*

[4] The day of the month is not given, but presumably it lay between the third and the fifteenth. Presumably, also, the play was licensed to the Cockpit Company, mentioned in the immediately preceding entry. It is not extant.

[5] Not extant.

[6] Not extant. Fleay, *B. C. E. D.* ii. 327: "The story of Robert, King Sicily, I suppose."

**1624, October 22.** "For the Palsgrave's Company; A new Play, called, *The Bristowe Merchant:*[1] Written by Forde, and Decker." (*S. A.* 219.)

**1624, November 3.** "For the Cockpit Company; A new Play, called, *The Parliament of Love:* Written by Massinger."[2] (*S. A.* 219; *Var.* iii. 230.)

**1624, November 3.** "For the Palsgrave's Company; A new Play, called, *The Masque.* The masque book was allowed of for the press; and was brought me by Mr. Jon[son] the 29th December 1624."[3] (*S. A.* 219.)

**1624, December.** [*The Spanish Viceroy* was acted without license, for which Herbert exacted from the players an apology. See page 21.]

**1624, December 29.** [See the entry above under November 3.]

**1624–5, January 25.** "For the Prince's Company; A new Play, called, *The Widow's Prize;*[4] which containing much abusive matter, was allowed of by me, on condition, that my reformations were observed." (*S. A.* 219–220.)

**1624–5, February 8.** "For the king's company. An olde play called *The Honest Man's Fortune*, the originall being lost, was re-allowed by mee at Mr. Taylor's intreaty, and on condition to give mee a booke [*The Arcadia*], this 8 Februa. 1624."[5] (*Var.* iii. 229.)

[1] Not extant. Fleay, *B. C. E. D.* i. 233, suggests that this is perhaps a refashioning of Day's *Bristol Tragedy*, bought by Henslowe in May, 1602.

[2] The play was entered S. R. June 29, 1660, as by William Rowley, and so appears in Warburton's list. The last four acts are preserved in the Dyce MS. 39.

[3] This entry seems to be confused. I should like to identify the "new play called *The Masque*" with the play entered in Warburton's list as "A Mask" by R. Govell. Since "R. Govell" is not otherwise heard of, I suspect that this is Warburton's reading of "R. Gunell," who was at this time the manager of the Palsgrave's Company and one of its chief playwrights (see the note to the license entry of December 4, 1623). For the latter part of the entry see page 41. "Mr. Jon" may be either Ben Jonson, or Inigo Jones; but Herbert seems to have used the spelling "Johnson" (see pp. 34, 50).

[4] Not extant. It was entered in S. R. September 9, 1653, as by William Sampson; and was listed by Warburton: "The Widows Prise, C[omedy], W^m. Sampson." Both Fleay and Greg, unable to find this license entry, questioned Halliwell's notice of it in his *Dictionary of Old Plays.*

[5] This is repeated by Chalmers, *S. A.* 220, but without the statement that the book referred to was the *Arcadia.* Malone adds the following comment: "The manuscript copy of *The Honest Man's Fortune* is now before me, and is dated 1613. It was therefore probably the joint production of Beaumont and Fletcher. This piece was acted at the Globe, and the copy which had been licensed by Sir George Buc, was without doubt destroyed by the fire which

**1624–5, February 11.** "For the Cockpit Company; A new Play, called, *Love-Tricks with Compliments*."[1] (*S. A.* 220; *Var.* iii. 231.)

**1625–6, January 22.** *The Fair Maid of the Inn*, by John Fletcher, licensed; acted at the Blackfriars. (*Var.* iii. 226.)

**1625–6, February 3.** *The Noble Gentleman*, by John Fletcher, licensed; acted at the Blackfriars. (*Var.* iii. 227.)

**1625–6, February 9.** *The Maid's Revenge*, by James Shirley, licensed. (*Var.* iii. 231.)

**1626, October 11.** *The Roman Actor*, by Philip Massinger, licensed for the King's Company. (*Var.* iii. 230.)

**1626, November 4.** *The Brothers*,[2] by James Shirley, licensed.

**1626–7, January 12.** *The Cruel Brother*, by William Davenant, licensed. (*Var.* iii. 284; 98.)

**1627, June 6.** *The Judge*, by Philip Massinger, licensed for the King's Company.[3] (*Var.* iii. 230.)

**1627, July 5.** *The Great Duke*[4] was licensed for the Queen's Servants, July 5, 1627. (*Var.* iii. 230.)

**1628, May 6.** *The Honour of Women*[5] was licensed May 6, 1628. (*Var.* iii. 230.)

consumed that theatre in the year 1613." Fleay contends that the play was written by Fletcher, Massinger, Field, and Daborne; that originally it was acted by the Lady Elizabeth's Men, not by the King's Men at the Globe; that Taylor "had probably kept the Lady Elizabeth's stage copy, and now sold it to the King's Men"—hence, perhaps, the gift of a book. See his *History of the Stage*, p. 305, and *B. C. E. D.* i. 195.

[1] *The School of Compliment*, by James Shirley. Malone, *Var.* iii. 231, gives the date as February 10.

[2] A play by Shirley with the title *The Brothers* was printed in 1652; but Fleay, *B. C. E. D.* ii. 236, 246, identifies the present play with *Dick of Devonshire*. See also the entry under 1641, May 26. (*Var.* iii. 231.)

[3] *The Judge, or Believe as You List*, was entered S. R. September 9, 1653. Since no judge appears in *Believe as You List* we may suspect that the publisher was attempting to smuggle two plays through for the fee of one. "The Judge, A C[omedy], by Phill. Massenger" appears in Warburton's list, and if possessed by that antiquarian was destroyed by his cook. Fleay, *B. C. E. D.* i. 208, 223, suggests that the play was probably an alteration of *The Fatal Dowry*.

[4] Malone adds: "This, I apprehend, was *The Great Duke of Florence*, which was acted by that company."

[5] Malone adds: "I suspect that this was the original name of *The Maid of Honour*, which was printed in 1631, though not entered for the stage in Sir Henry Herbert's book." We find entered in S. R. September 9, 1653, *The Spanish Viceroy, or The Honour of Women*. The King's Men had performed *The Spanish Viceroy* in 1624 without license (see page 21), and possibly that play was now officially licensed under a new title. It may be, however,

**1628, October 3.** *The Witty Fair One*, by James Shirley, licensed. (*Var.* iii. 231.)

**1628, November 24.** Ford's play [*The Lovers' Melancholy*] was exhibited at the Blackfriars on the 24th of November, 1628, when it was licensed for the stage,[1] as appears from the office-book of Sir Henry Herbert, Master of the Revels to King Charles the First, a manuscript now before me . . . and Jonson's New Inn on the 19th of January in the following year, 1628-9. (*Var.* i. 421.)

**1628-9, January 19.** *The New Inn*, by Ben Jonson, licensed.[2] (*Var.* i. 421.)

**1628-9, February 9.** Very soon, indeed, after the ill success of Jonson's piece [*The New Inn*], the King's Company brought out at the same theatre [Blackfriars] a new play called *The Love-sick Maid, or the Honour of Young Ladies*,[3] which was licensed by Sir Henry Herbert on the 9th of February, 1628-9, and acted with extraordinary applause. This play, which was written by Jonson's own servant, Richard Brome, was so popular, that the managers of the King's Company, on the 10th of March, presented the Master of the Revels with the sum of two pounds, "on the good success of *The Honour of Ladies;*" the only instance I have met with of such a compliment being paid him. (*Var.* i. 421.)

**1629, May 13.** "For allowing of a new act in an ould play, this 13th of May, 1629,—£o. 10. o." (*Var.* i. 424.)

**1629, June 8.** *The Picture*, by Philip Massinger, licensed for the King's Company. (*Var.* iii. 230.)

**1629, July 22.** *The Colonel*, by William Davenant, licensed. (*Var.* iii. 284.)

**1629, July 29.** *The Northern Lass*, which was acted by the King's Company on the 29th of July, 1629.[4] (*Var.* i. 431; 419.)

**1629, October 2.** *The Just Italian*, by William Davenant, licensed. (*Var.* iii. 284.)

that the publisher was attempting to smuggle two separate plays through for a single fee. In Warburton's list we read: "The Hon<sup>r</sup>. of Women, A C[omedy]. by Massinger." Presumably the MS. was destroyed by his cook.

[1] Malone seems to have assumed that plays were acted on the day they were licensed. See page 19, 1632, November 18 and note; page 20, 1633, October 18; page 32, 1629, July 29; page 36, 1634, November 24.

[2] See the license entry of 1628, November 24.

[3] Not extant. It was entered in S. R. on September 9, 1653.

[4] Malone apparently derived this information from the office-book of Herbert which he had before him. Fleay, *B. C. E. D.* i. 36, on internal evidence, says: "written after Nov. 1630."

**1629, November 3.** *Minerva's Sacrifice*,[1] by Philip Massinger, licensed for the King's Company. (*Var.* iii. 230.)

**1629, November 3.** *The Faithful Servant*,[2] by James Shirley, licensed. (*Var.* iii. 231.)

**1630–1, January 11.** [Herbert refused to license a play by Massinger; see page 19.]

**1630–1, March 11.** *The Emperor of the East*, by Philip Massinger, licensed for the King's Company.[3] (*Var.* iii. 230.)

**1631, May 4.** *The Traitor*, by James Shirley, licensed. (*Var.* iii. 231.)

**1631, May 7 [6?].** *Believe as You List*, by Philip Massinger, licensed for the King's Company.[4] (*Var.* iii. 230.)

**1631, May 17.** *The Duke*,[5] by James Shirley, licensed. (*Var.* iii. 232.)

**1631, June 13.** *The Unfortunate Piety*,[6] by Philip Massinger, licensed for the King's Company. (*Var.* iii. 230.)

**1631, November 14.** *Love's Cruelty*, by James Shirley, licensed. (*Var.* iii. 232.)

**1631, December.** [*Holland's Leaguer*, by Shackerley Marmion, was acted at Salisbury Court; see page 45.]

**1631–2, January 10.** *The Changes*, by James Shirley, licensed.[7] (*Var.* iii. 232.)

[1] Not extant. Fleay incorrectly gives the date as "November 23." *Minerva's Sacrifice, or The Forced Lady*, by Massinger, was entered S. R. on September 9, 1653; *The Forced Lady*, a tragedy, by Massinger, was entered S. R. on June 29, 1660; *Minerva's Sacrifice*, by Phill. Masenger, was entered in Warburton's list. Fleay, *B. C. E. D.* i. 32, 206, suggests that it was *The Queen of Corinth* altered by Massinger.
[2] Published in 1630 as *The Grateful Servant*.
[3] Fleay incorrectly gives the date as "Mar. 20."
[4] The original MS. of the play is now in the British Museum with Herbert's license at the end: "This Play, called Believe as You liste, may bee acted, this 6 day of May, 1631. Henry Herbert." For a discussion of the MS. see *The Athenæum*, January 19, 1901. Though the license itself is dated May 6, probably Herbert did not deliver the play to the actors until the following day, hence the entry in his office-book of May 7. By Fleay and others the play is thought to be a revision of the play containing "the deposition of Sebastian King of Portugal by Philip the Second," which on January 11 Herbert had refused to license; see page 19.
[5] Fleay, *B. C. E. D.* ii. 237, identifies this with *The Humorous Courtier*.
[6] *The Unfortunate Piety, or The Italian Nightpiece* was entered S. R. on September 9, 1653. Fleay identifies the play with *The Double Marriage*, and also *The Tyrant*; see *B. C. E. D.* i. 210–211; 225.
[7] The play was entered on the Stationer's Registers on February 9, 1631–32, and was printed shortly after "as it was presented at the private house in Salisbury Court, by the company of His Majestie's Revels." But His

**1632, April 20.**   *Hyde Park*, by James Shirley, licensed.   (*Var.* iii. 232.)

**1632, May 25.**   *The City Madam*, by Philip Massinger, licensed for the King's Company.   (*Var.* iii. 230; 112.)

**1632, October 12.**   "Received of Knight,[1] for allowing of Ben Johnsons play called *Humours Reconcil'd, or the Magnetick Lady*, to bee acted, this 12th of Octob. 1632, 2*l.* o. o."   (*Var.* iii. 231.)

**1632, November 16.**   *The Ball*, by James Shirley, licensed.[2]   (*Var.* iii. 232.)

**1632–3, January 21.**   *The Bewties*,[3] by James Shirley, licensed.   (*Var.* iii. 232.)

**1632–3, March.**   Soon after his father's death he [William Heminges] commenced a dramatick poet, having produced in March, 1632–3, a comedy entitled *The Coursinge of a Hare, or the Madcapp*, which was performed at the Fortune theatre,[4] but is now lost.   MS. Herbert.   (*Var.* iii. 189.)

**1633, May 7.**   "R. for allowinge of *The Tale of the Tubb*, Vitru Hoop's parte wholly strucke out, and the motion of the tubb, by commande from my lorde chamberlin; exceptions being taken against it by Inigo Jones, surveyor of the kings workes, as a personal injury unto him.[5]   May 7, 1633,—2*l.* o. o."   (*Var.* iii. 232.)

**1633, May 11.**   "For a play of Fletchers corrected by Sherley, called *The Night Walkers*,[6] the 11 May, 1633,—£2. o. o.   For the queen's players."   (*Var.* iii. 236; i. 424.)

**1633, June 27.**   [On the last page of the MS. of William Methold's *The Launching of the May, or The Seaman's Honest Wife* (MS. Egerton 1994), is the following license: "This Play, called y^e Seamans Honest wife, all y^e Oaths left out in Y^e action as they are crost in y^e booke, & all other Reformations strictly

Majesty's Revels left Salisbury Court in December, 1631.   Possibly Malone should have given the date of license as January 10, 1630–31.   For further discussion see Adams, *Shakespearean Playhouses*, pp. 376–78.

[1] The book-keeper of the King's Men.

[2] Yet on November 18 Herbert objected to the play; see page 19.

[3] Fleay, *B. C. E. D.* ii. 239, says: "Beyond doubt the same as *The Bird in a Cage*."

[4] Yet he was one of the housekeepers at the Globe, having inherited his father's shares.   His extant plays are *The Fatal Contract* and *The Jews' Tragedy*.   A[ndrew] P[ennycuicke], and A[nthony] T[urner], who published *The Fatal Contract* in 1653, speak of other important works by Heminges.

[5] The play was given at Court on January 14, 1633–4, and "not likte"; see page 54.

[6] Performed at Court on January 30, 1633–4, and "likt as a merry play."

observ'd, may bee acted, not otherwyse. This 27. June. 1633.
Henry Herbert. I commande your Bookeeper to present mee
with a faire Copy hereafter and to leave out all oathes, prophaness, & publick Ribaldry, as he will answer it at his perill
Herbert."]

**1633, July 3.** *The Young Admiral*, by James Shirley, licensed.[1]
(*Var.* iii. 232.)

**1633, August 15.** "Received of Biston,[2] for an ould play
called *Hymen's Holliday*,[3] newly revived at their house, being a
play given unto him for my use, this 15 Aug. 1633, 3*l.* o. o.
Received of him for some alterations in it 1*l.* o. o." (*Var.* iii.
233.)

**1633, October.** [*The Citty Shuffler* licensed for Salisbury
Court; see page 20.]

**1633, October 31.** *The Guardian*, by Philip Massinger,
licensed for the King's Company.[4] (*Var.* iii. 230.)

**1633, November 11.** *The Gamester*, by James Shirley,
licensed.[5] (*Var.* iii. 232.)

**1633, November 23.** "The Kings players sent me an ould
booke[6] of Fletchers called *The Loyal Subject*, formerly allowed
by Sir George Bucke, 16 Novemb. 1618, which according to
their desire and agreement I did peruse, and with some reformations allowed of, the 23 of Nov. 1633, for which they sent mee
according to their promise 1*l.* o. o." (*Var.* iii. 234.)

**1633-4, January 19.** *The Wits*, by William Davenant,
licensed.[7] (*Var.* iii. 284.)

**1634, May 7.** The tragedy of *Cleander*, by Philip Massinger,
was licensed for the King's Company.[8] (*Var.* iii. 230.)

[1] For Herbert's praise of this play see page 19. It was performed at Court
on November 19, and "likt by the K. and Queen."
[2] Christopher Beeston, manager of the Cockpit in Drury Lane.
[3] "On Monday night the 16 of December, 1633, at Whitehall, was acted
before the King and Queen, *Hymens Holliday or Cupids Fegarys*, an ould play
of Rowleys. Likte."—(*Var.* iii. 234.) It had been previously acted at Court
on February 24, 1612. Fleay contends that William and not Samuel Rowley
was the author.
[4] It was acted at Court on the following January 12.
[5] For an interesting note on the play, see page 54.
[6] Malone states that Herbert wrote in the margin "The first ould play
sent mee to be perused by the K. players." It was presented at Court on
December 16.
[7] For Herbert's severe censorship of the play, and Davenant's appeal to
the king, see page 22. See also Herbert's comment when the play was acted
at Court on January 28, 1633-4.
[8] The play is not extant; Fleay, however, seeks to identify it with *The
Wandering Lovers*; see the note under the license entry 1623, December.

**1634, June 6.**  *A Very Woman*, by Philip Massinger, licensed for the King's Company.  (*Var.* iii. 230.)

**1634, June 24.**  *The Example*, by James Shirley, licensed. (*Var.* iii. 232.)

**1634, August 16.**  "An ould play, with some new scenes, Doctor Lambe and the Witches, to Salisbury Court, the 16th August, 1634,—£1. 0. 0."  (*Var.* i. 424.)

**1634, November 20.**  *Love and Honour*, by William Davenant, licensed.[1]  (*Var.* iii. 284.)

**1634, November 24.**  *The Proxy, or Love's Aftergame*, was produced at the theatre at Salisbury Court, November 24, 1634.[2] (*Var.* iii. 238.)

**1634, November 29.**  *The Opportunity*, by James Shirley, licensed.  (*Var.* iii. 232.)

**1634-5, January 10.**  *The Orator*, by Philip Massinger, licensed for the King's Company.[3]  (*Var.* iii. 230.)

**1634-5, February 6.**  *The Coronation*, by James Shirley, licensed.[4]  (*Var.* iii. 232.)

**1635, April 29.**  *Chabot, Admiral of France*, by George Chapman and James Shirley, licensed.  (*Var.* iii. 232.)

**1635, August 1.**  *News of Plymouth*, by William Davenant, licensed.  (*Var.* iii. 284.)

**1635, September 16.**  "Received of Blagrove from the King's Company, for the renewing of *Love's Pilgrimage*,[5] the 16th of September, 1635,—£1. 0. 0."  (*Var.* i. 424.)

---

[1] Malone adds the information: "*Love and Honour* was originally called *The Courage of Love*. It was afterwards named by Sir Henry Herbert, at D'Avenant's request, *The Nonpareilles, or the Matchless Maids.*" It was acted at Court on January 1, 1636-7.

[2] This is the source of Halliwell's statement, *Dictionary of Old Plays*, p. 202, which Fleay could not discover; see *B. C. E. D.* ii. 336. The play is not extant, although it was entered S. R. on November 29, 1653. It was acted at Court February 24, 1635-6.

[3] *The Noble Choice, or y^e Orator* was entered by Mosely in S. R. on September 9, 1653, as by Massinger. "The Noble Choice, T[ragi] C[omedy] P. Massinger" appears in Warburton's list. It is possible that Mosely was attempting to smuggle two plays through for a single fee. The play is not extant; Fleay, *B. C. E. D.* i. 228, suggests that it was "only a reformation" of *The Elder Brother*.

[4] This play was printed in 1640 as by Beaumont and Fletcher, but was claimed by Shirley in 1652. It was reprinted in the 1679 folio of Beaumont and Fletcher.

[5] Fleay, who could not find this passage in Malone, incorrectly writes: "Malone says that this play" is "stated in Herbert's MS. to have been left imperfect by Fletcher and finished by Shirley." But Malone said no such

**1635, October 15.** *The Lady of Pleasure*, by James Shirley, licensed. (*Var.* iii. 232.)

**1635, October 15.** [Affixed to the MS. of Glapthorne's *Lady Mother*, now preserved in the British Museum, is the following license signed by Herbert's deputy: "This Play, call'd the Lady Mother (the Reformacons observ'd) may be acted. October the xvth, 1635. Will Blagrave, Dept. to the Master of the Revells."]

**1635, November 16.** *The Platonic Lovers*, by William Davenant, licensed. (*Var.* iii. 284.)

**1635-6, January 18.** *The Duke's Mistress*, by James Shirley, licensed.[1] (*Var.* iii. 232.)

**1636, May 9.** *The Bashful Lover*, by Philip Massinger, licensed for the King's Company.[2] (*Var.* iii. 230.)

**1636, May 12.** "Received of ould Cartwright[3] for allowing the [Fortune] company to add scenes to an ould play, and to give it out for a new one,[4] this 12th of May, 1636,—£1. 0. 0." (*Var.* i. 424.)

**1638, April 16.** *The Unfortunate Lovers*, by William Davenant, licensed. (*Var.* iii. 284.)

**1638, April 23.** *The Royal Master*, by James Shirley, licensed. (*Var.* iii. 232.)

**1638, May 3.** One of the leaves of Sir Henry Herbert's Manuscript, which was missing, having been recovered since

thing. Fleay adds, *B. C. E. D.* i. 193: "This alteration was no doubt the transference of a considerable part of i, 1 from *The New Inn*, which had been hissed off the stage in 1629, and published in 1631. The alteration was, of course, made by Jonson."

[1] It was acted at Court on February 22.

[2] *Alexis the Chaste Gallant, or The Bashful Lover*, by Massinger, was entered in S. R. Sept. 9, 1653; *The Bashful Lover*, by Massinger, was printed in 1655; *Alexias or Ye Chast Gallant*, by Massinger, appears in Warburton's list of MS. plays; *Alexius, or the Chaste Lover* was licensed by Herbert on Sept. 25, 1639, for the King's company; *Alexius*, by Massinger, is mentioned in a list of plays of the King's Men in 1641, found in one of the Lord Chamberlain's Warrant Books (see The Malone Society's *Collections*, i. 366); *Alice and Alexis* is the title of a fragment of an early seventeenth century comedy, in the Bodleian Library (*Douce MS.* 171, f. 48ᵛ). It is probable that the entry in the S. R. was a device to license two plays for a single fee, and that *Alexius* has perished—possibly at the hands of Warburton's cook.

[3] William Cartwright, the actor; he is mentioned in the royal patent issued January 11, 1613, to the Fortune company.

[4] "The players are as crafty with an old play as bauds with old faces, the one puts on a new fresh colour, the other a new face and name." Donald Lupton, *London and The Countrey Carbonadoed and Quartered*, 1632. "New titles warrant not a play for new." Prologue to *The False One*.

the remark in the text was made, I find that the *Ladies Trial* [1]
was performed for the first time at the Cockpit theatre in May,
1638, on the 3d of which month it was licensed by the Master
of the Revels.   (*Var.* i. 424.)

**1638, June 5.**   "Received of Mr. Lowens for my paines about
Messinger's play called *The King and the Subject*, 2 June, 1638,
1*l.* 0. 0.
"The name of *The King and the Subject* is altered, and I
allowed the play to bee acted, the reformations most strictly
observed,[2] and not otherwise, the 5th of June, 1638."   (*Var.* iii.
240.)

**1638, November 17.**   *The Fair Favourite*, by William Davenant, licensed.[3]   (*Var.* iii. 284.)

**1639, September 25.**   *Alexius, or The Chaste Lover*, by Philip
Massinger, licensed for the King's Company.[4]   (*Var.* iii. 231.)

**1639, October 30.**   *The Gentleman of Venise*, by James Shirley,
licensed.[5]   (*Var.* iii. 232.)

**1639, November 30.**   *The Spanish Lovers*, by William Davenant, licensed.[6]   (*Var.* iii. 284.)

**1639–40, January 26.**   *The Fair Anchoress of Pausilippo,*[7]
by Philip Massinger,[8] licensed for the King's Company.   (*Var.*
iii. 231.)

[1] By John Ford.  Fleay, who did not know of this Herbert entry, concluded
from internal evidence that the play was acted "after 17th Aug. 1637."
[2] For an interesting commentary by Herbert on the play, with a quotation,
and a comment by the king, see pages 22–23.  Malone says (*Var.* iii. 230):
"*The King and the Subject*, June 5, 1638.  Acted by the same company.  This
title, Sir Henry Herbert says, was changed.  I suspect it was new named *The
Tyrant*.  The play is lost."  A play called *The Tyrant* was entered in S. R.
June 29, 1660, but was not printed.  In Warburton's list we find "The Tyrant,
A Tragedy by Phill. Massenger."  The MS. was advertised in Warburton's
sale, November, 1759, but I am not able to discover its present owner.  Fleay,
*B. C. E. D.* i. 211, seeks to identify the play with *The Double Marriage*,
although in the same volume, page 229, he identifies it with *The King and the
Subject*.  Phelan, *Anglia*, ii. 47, seeks to identify it with *The Second Maiden's
Tragedy*.
[3] "The fair favourit" appears in Warburton's list without any author's
name; it was published in Davenant's works, folio, 1673.
[4] See the note to *The Bashful Lover*, licensed 1636, May 9.
[5] The date is correctly given in the 1790 Malone; by an error the *Variorum*
gives the year as 1629.  See the note to *The Renegade*, 1624, April 17.
[6] Malone adds: "This piece is probably the play which in his works is
called *The Distresses*."
[7] Not extant.  In S. R., September 9, 1653, we find entered *The Prisoner,
or The Fair Anchoress*, by Philip Massinger;  and on June 29, 1660, *The
Prisoners*, T-C., by Massinger.  In 1664 Killigrew printed a play entitled
*The Prisoners*.  It is possible that in the first Stationers' Register entry the
publisher was attempting to smuggle two plays through for a single fee.
[8] This is the last time that Massinger appears in the office-book.  Malone

**1640, June 1.** *Rosania*, by James Shirley, licensed. (*Var.* iii. 232.)

**1640, November 10.** *The Impostor*,[2] by James Shirley, licensed. (*Var.* iii. 232.)

**1641, May 26.** *The Politique Father*,[3] by James Shirley, licensed. (*Var.* iii. 232.)

**1641, November 25.** *The Cardinal*, by James Shirley, licensed. (*Var.* iii. 232.)

**1642, April 26.** *The Sisters*, by James Shirley, licensed. (*Var.* iii. 232.)

**1642, June 8.** "Received of Mr. Kirke,[4] for a new play which I burnte for the ribaldry and offense that was in it, 2*l*. 0. 0.

"Received of Mr. Kirke for another new play called *The Irishe Rebellion*,[5] the 8 June, 1642, 2*l*. 0. 0." (*Var.* iii. 241–242.)

"Here ended my allowance of plaies, for the war began in Aug. 1642." (*Var.* iii. 242.)

## III.  LICENSES FOR THE PRESS

Although Tilney asserted the right of the Office of the Revels to license plays for acting, his deputy, Sir George Buc, seems first to have asserted the right of the Office to license plays for printing. The importance of the Master in this capacity after the year 1607, when Buc assumed full charge of the Office, is clearly

notes that *The Fatal Dowry* and *A New Way to Pay Old Debts* do "not appear to have been licensed for the stage" by Herbert, at least under those titles; and of *The Spanish Viceroy* he notes that it was "acted in 1624" (*Var.* iii. 230).

[1] The play was acted in Ogilby's Dublin theatre with the alternative title *Loves Victory*. Before August 7, 1641, its title was changed to *The Doubtful Heir*; see The Malone Society's *Collections*, i. 366. It was printed in 1652 as *The Doubtful Heir*.

[2] Printed in 1652 as *The Imposture*.

[3] Some have thought this *The Politician*, printed in 1655; Fleay, *B. C. E. D.* ii. 246, says: "It is certainly the play published as *The Brothers*" in 1652, and this seems to be correct.

[4] John Kirke, who published in 1638 *The Seven Champions of Christendom*, as it was acted at the Cockpit and at the Red Bull. In 1637 he published Henry Shirley's *The Martyred Soldier* with a dedication to Sir Kenelm Digby. Little else is known of him.

[5] Not extant.

revealed by Fleay's tables based on the Stationers' Register. Miss Gildersleeve has admirably summed up the facts as follows:

On November 21, 1606, Buc appears in the Stationers' Register as licenser of the *Fleare*, a comedy. Several plays are then entered under other license; but on April 10, 1607, Buc appears again, and from now on until 1615 every play except two was entered under the license of the Master or his Deputy. He had evidently almost established his authority as sole censor of printed plays. But as Buc's energy waned with his advancing years, the administration of the Revels Office apparently grew lax, and a considerable number of plays appeared under other license. As Herbert developed his business, however, he re-established this authority, and from 1628 to 1637 he or his Deputy licensed every play entered in the Stationers' Register. After January 29, 1638, the Revels license appears no more,—perhaps as a result of Archbishop Laud's new regulations concerning the censorship of the press.

Herbert's eagerness to re-establish his authority over the printing of plays is indicated by the following note in Arber's reprint of the Stationers' Register:[2]

One of the Company having entered in the Register a play without license, immediately, at the instigation of Sir Henry Herbert, the Clerk was prohibited from entering any "plays, tragedies, tragic comedies, or pastoralls," without the authority of the Master of the Revels.

Herbert claimed also the right to license poetry in general. On one occasion, at least, this brought him into trouble, for on November 14, 1632, the Star Chamber ordered "Sir Henry Herbert to give account on the same day why he warranted the book of Dr. Dun's [Donne's] Paradoxes to be printed."[3]

Below I have arranged the notices of Herbert's licenses for the press as cited from his office-book by Malone and Chalmers.

[1] *Government Regulation of the Elizabethan Drama*, p. 84.
[2] Vol. v, page lv. Arber does not give the date.
[3] *Calendar of State Papers, Domestic, 1631–1633*, p. 437.

This [Massinger's *Noble Bondman*] was allowed to be printed on the 12th March, 1624. (*S. A.* 216.)[1]

"The masque book [of *Pan's Anniversary?*] was allowed of for the press; and was brought me by Mr. Jon[son][2] the 29th December 1624." (*S. A.* 219.)

And, the master of the Revels appears also to have licensed books, during the reigns of King James, and Charles the 1st; he received a fee, for allowing Ovid's *Epistles*, translated into English; he received a fee, for a book of verses of my Lord Brook's, called *Coelia;* he received of Sayle, the Bookbinder, *ten* shillings, for allowing to be printed two other small pieces of verses, done by *a boy* of *thirteen*, called *Cowley*. (*S. A.* 209-210.)

Immediately after this entry is another, which accounts for the defect of several leaves in the edition of Lord Brooke's *Poems*, 1633: "Received from Henry Seyle for allowinge a booke of verses of my lord Brooks, entitled *Religion, Humane Learning, Warr, and Honor,* this 17 of October 1632, in mony, 1*l.* 0*s.* 0*d.* in books to the value of 1*l.* 4*s.* 0*d.*"—In all the published copies twenty leaves on the subject of Religion, are wanting, having been cancelled, probably, by the order of Archbishop Laud.

The subsequent entry ascertains the date of Cowley's earliest production:

"More of Seyle, for allowinge of two other small peeces of verses for the press, done by a boy of this town called Cowley, at the same time, 0*l.* 10*s.* 0*d.*" (*Var.* iii. 231.)

"The pastorall of *Florimene*, (says Sir Henry) with the description of the sceanes and interludes, as it was sent mee by Mr. Inigo Jones, I allowed for the press, this 14 of Decemb. 1635. The pastorall is in French, and 'tis the argument only, put into English, that I have allowed to be printed." (*Var.* iii. 122.)

*Britannia Triumphans* licensed for press, Jan. 8, 1637. (*Var.* iii. 284.)[3]

---

[1] Chalmers apparently records this from Herbert's office-book. I find the play entered in the Stationers' Register on March 12, 1624, as licensed by Herbert.

[2] So Chalmers expands the abbreviation; but Herbert may have intended to refer to Inigo Jones; see p. 30, note 3.

[3] By Davenant. The masque, as the title-page states, was presented "at Whitehall by the King's Majestie and his Lords, on the Sunday after Twelfth-night, 1637," i. e. on January 7, 1637–8.

At the Restoration Herbert sought to re-establish his authority to license plays and poetry; and on July 25, 1663, his deputy, Edward Hayward, drew up an elaborate document entitled "Arguments to prove that the Master of his Maiesties Office of the Revells hath not onely the power of Lycencing all playes, Poems, and ballads, but of appointing them to the Press." This document, printed on page 125, should be read in connection with the present chapter.

## IV. LICENSES OF PLAYHOUSES AND COMPANIES

Tilney, as we have seen, established the right of the Office of the Revels to license the erection of play-houses, and to charge the companies an annual fee for allowance. Herbert positively declared in 1660 that "no person or persons have erected any playhouse, or raised any company of players without license" from his predecessors or himself. In his office-book he transcribed from the records of Sir George Buc, apparently to serve as a precedent, the following entry:

"July 13, 1613, for a license to erect a new play-house in the White-friers, &c. £20." (*Var.* iii. 52.)[1]

Licenses for erecting new playhouses, however, were few, and Herbert must have found a more profitable source of income in allowing the companies to operate the playhouses already in existence. Different companies seem to have paid him for this allowance in different ways. The King's Company, occupying the Globe in the summer and the Blackfriars in the winter,

[1] Probably granted to Rosseter or Henslowe or both for a theatre to house the Lady Elizabeth's Men; see Adams, *Shakespearean Playhouses*, chapters on the Whitefriars and the Hope.

gave him a summer and a winter benefit performances:

"The kinges company with a generall consent and alacritye have given mee the benefitt of too dayes in the yeare, the one in summer, thother in winter, to bee taken out of the second daye of a revived playe, att my owne choyse. The housekeepers have likewyse given their shares, their dayly charge only deducted, which comes to some 2*l*. 5*s*. this 25 May, 1628.[2]

"The benefitt of the first day, being a very unseasonable one in respect of the weather, comes but unto £4. 15. 0."

This agreement subsisted for five years and a half, during which time Sir Henry Herbert had ten benefits, the most profitable of which produced seventeen pounds, and ten shillings, *net*, on the 22d of Nov. 1628, when Fletcher's *Custom of the Country* was performed at Blackfriars; and the least emolument which he received was on the representation of a play which is not named, at the Globe, in the summer of the year 1632, which produced only the sum of one pound and five shillings, after deducting from the total receipt in each instance the nightly charge above mentioned.[3] I shall give below the receipt taken by him on each of the ten performances; from which it appears that his clear profit at an average on each of his nights,[3] was £8. 19. 4. and the total nightly receipt was at an average—£11. 4. 4.

1628.　　May 25, [the play not named,]—4*l*. 15*s*. 0*d*.
　　　　　　"The benefitt of the winters day, being the second daye of an old play called *The Custome of the Cuntrye*, came to 17*l*. 10*s*. 0*d*. this 22 of Nov. 1628. From the Kinges company att the Blackfryers.

1629.　　"The benefitt of the summers day from the kinges company, being brought mee by Blagrave,[4] upon the play of *The Prophetess*, comes to, this 21 of July, 1629,—6*l*. 7*s*. 0*d*.

[1] Chalmers incorrectly states (*Apology*, p. 520) that all the playhouses gave Herbert a winter and a summer benefit. When Chalmers wrote this he had not seen the Herbert MSS., and must have based his statement on the passages quoted by Malone, and printed below.

[2] Fleay, *History of the Stage*, p. 333, says "Query, £820 per annum." What he means I cannot imagine. The housekeepers were the owners of the Globe and Blackfriars buildings, who received each day a certain share of the takings. They agreed to give this share to Herbert, the daily charge of sweeping, etc., deducted; on May 25, 1628, the amount he received from the housekeepers was £2 5*s*. Whether this was in addition to the £4 15*s* mentioned in the next sentence, or a part of it is not clear.

[3] Malone seems to have forgotten that the performances were in the afternoon. The charge mentioned was "the dayly charge."

[4] William Blagrove, Herbert's deputy: in the summer of this year he joined Gunell in erecting the Salisbury Court Playhouse.

"The benefitt of the winters day from the kinges company being brought mee by Blagrave, upon the play of *The Moor of Venise*, comes, this 22 of Nov. 1629, unto—9*l*. 16*s*. 0*d*.

1630.    [*No play this summer on account of the plague.*]

"Received of Mr. Taylor and Lowins, in the name of their company, for the benefitt of my winter day, upon the second day of Ben Jonson's play of *Every Man in his Humour*, this 18 day of February, 1630 [1630–31]—12*l*. 4*s*. 0*d*.

1631.    "Received of Mr. Shanke, in the name of the kings company, for the benefitt of their summer day, upon y⁰ second daye of *Richard y⁰ Seconde*, at the Globe, this 12 of June, 1631,—5*l*. 6*s*. 6*d*.

"Received of Mr. Blagrave, in the name of the kings company, for the benefitt of my winter day, taken upon *The Alchemiste*, this 1 of Decemb. 1631,—13*l*. 0*s*. 0*d*.[1]

1632.    "Received for the summer day of the kings company y⁰ 6 Novemb. 1632,[2]—1*l*. 5*s*. 0*d*.

"Received for the winter day upon *The Wild Goose Chase*, y⁰ same day,—15*l*. 0*s*. 0*d*.

1633.    "R. of y⁰ kings company, for my summers day, by Blagrave, the 6 of June 1633, y⁰ somme of 4*l*. 10*s*. 0*d*." (*Var*. iii. 176–177.)

On the 30th of October, 1633, the managers of the king's company agreed to pay him the fixed sum of ten pounds every Christmas, and the same sum at Midsummer, in lieu of his two benefits, which sums they regularly paid him from that time till the breaking out of the civil wars. (*Var*. iii. 177–178; cf. *Apology*, p. 520.)

In view of this it is somewhat surprising to find that in 1662 Herbert, in "a remembrance of the fees" he formerly received, claimed:[3]

---

[1] In this year Herbert seems to have received a third benefit for some special service rendered the company:

"Received of Mr. Benfielde, in the name of the kings company, for a gratuity for ther liberty gaind unto them of playinge, upon the cessation of the plague, this 10 of June, 1631,—3*l*. 10*s*. 0*d*."—"This (Sir Henry Herbert adds) was taken upon *Pericles* at the Globe." (*Var*. iii. 177.)

[2] The date is given correctly in the 1790 Malone; the *Variorum* prints in error "1631."

[3] See p. 121.

The profittes of a summer's day play at the Blackfryers, valued at }  50    00    00

The profitts of a winter's day, at Black-fryers }  50    00    00

In the same document he informs us that "four companies of players (besides the late King's company)" gave him each, instead of benefit performances, a share in their profits.

For a share from each company of four companyes of players (besides the late Kinges Company) valued at a 100*l.* a yeare, one yeare with another, besides the usuall fees, by the yeare............. }  400    00    00

In still another document he proposes:

To prove a share payd by the Fortune Plaiers, and a share by the Bull Plaiers, and a share by Salsbery Court Players.[1]

This explains the following fact, which Malone misinterpreted:

The play of *Holland's Leaguer* was acted six days successively at Salisbury Court, in December, 1631, and yet Sir Henry Herbert received on account of the six representations but *one pound nineteen shillings*, in virtue of the *ninth* share which he possessed as one of the proprietors of that house. (*Var.* iii. 178.)

There is some evidence to show that the Cockpit Players, at one time, at least, instead of giving Herbert a share in their profits, paid him a fixed sum annually:

To prove that Mister Beeston [the manager of the Cockpit Playhouse] payd me 60*li.* per annum, besides usuall Fees, & allowances for Court plaies.[2]

[1] See p. 101.
[2] See p. 101. For Herbert's licensing of playhouses and companies at the Restoration see pp. 81, 84, 89, 93, 101.

## V.  LICENSES OF MUSICIANS

From Sir Henry Herbert's Manuscript I learn, that the musicians belonging to Shakspeare's company were obliged to pay the Master of the Revels an annual fee for a license[1] to play in the theatre.  (*Var.* iii. 112.)

"For a warrant to the Musitions of the King's company, this 9th of April, 1627,—£1. o. o."  *MS. Herbert.*  (*Var.* iii. 112.)

## VI.  LICENSES OF MISCELLANEOUS SHOWS

During the administration of Sir Henry Herbert, the Master of the Revels, as appears from his Official Register, exercised not only a peculiar jurisdiction over the stage, the plays, and the players, but also an unlimited authority over every other *show;* whether natural, or artificial; whether of trick, or ingenuity.[2] (*S. A.* 208.)

Sir Henry Herbert granted, on the 20th August 1623, a license *gratis*, to John Williams,[3] and four others, to make *showe* of *an Elephant*,[4] for a year; on the 5th of September to make showe of a *live Beaver;* On the 9th of June 1638, to make showe of an outlandish creature, called a *Possum;* a license to a Dutchman to show two *Dromedaries*,[5] for a year, for which, the licenser

---

[1] This right to license musicians Herbert attempted to re-establish at the Restoration.  "Whether particular musitians are not to bee lycenced aswell as companies, for that if they bee left free they may gather into companies without a Commission, and the Master may loose his fees"; see p. 127.  "To have a generall warrant for musick throughout England"; see p. 134.  Miss Gildersleeve, *Government Regulation of the Elizabethan Drama*, p. 70, thinks that Malone was mistaken, and that the warrant quoted above was merely a protection from arrest.  But Malone was probably correct in stating that Herbert licensed musicians to play.

[2] For his efforts to re-establish this jurisdiction after the Restoration see pp. 106, 123, 126, 130–39.

[3] This is probably the John Williams who with John Cotton and Thomas Dixon secured in 1620 a license from King James to build an amphitheatre "intended principally for martial exercises."  Again in 1626, with Thomas Dixon, he attempted to secure a somewhat similar license from King Charles. In both cases he was unsuccessful.  See Adams, *Shakespearean Playhouses.*

[4] Elephants were frequently put on exhibition; see Sir John Davies, ed. Grosart, pp. 318, 334; Marlowe, ed. Bullen, iii. 217; Jonson, ed. in 3 vols., i. 119.  Williams's elephant is probably referred to in Middleton's *Spanish Gipsie* (ed. Bullen, vi. 155, 188), written in this year.

[5] Possibly referred to, along with the elephant, in Middleton's *Spanish Gipsie* (ed. Bullen, vi. 155, 188):

> We no camels have to show,
> Nor elephant with growt head.

received one pound; a warrant to Grimes, for showing *the Camell:*—On the 14th of August 1624, a license was granted to Edward James to sett forth a *Showing Glass*, called the *World's Wonder:* On the 27th of August 1623, a license was granted to Barth. Cloys with three Assistants to make show of a *Musical Organ*, with divers motions in it;[1] to make show of an *Italian Motion;* to show *a Looking Glass;*[2] to show the *Philosopher's Lanthorn;* to show *a Virginal:*—A license was granted to Henry Momford, and others, "for tumbling, and vaulting, with *other tricks of slight of hand;*" for *a prize*[3] at the Bull by Mr. Allen, and Mr. Lewkner; to William Sands and others to show "the *Chaos of the World;*"[4] to show a motion called *the Creation of the World;*[5] to show certain *freaks* of *charging* and *discharging a gun;*[6] a license to Mr. Lowins, on the 18th of February 1630, for allowing of *a Dutch vaulter*, at their Houses, [the Globe, and Blackfriars.] A warrant was given to Francis Nicolini, an Italian, and his Company, "to dance on the ropes, to use *Interludes*, and *masques*, "and to *sell his powders, and balsams:*"— to John Puncteus, a Frenchman, professing *Physick*, with ten in his Company, to exercise *the quality of playing*, for a year, and to *sell his drugs:* On the 6th of March, a license was given *gratis* to Alexander Kukelson to teach the *art* of *musick* and *dancing*, for one year; A license to Thomas Gibson, to make shew of *pictures in Wax.*[7]   (*S. A.* 208–209.)

## VII. LENTEN DISPENSATIONS

Plays in the time of King James the First, (and probably afterwards,) appear to have been performed every day at each theatre during the winter season, except in the time of Lent, when they were not permitted on the sermon days, as they were called, that is, on Wednesday and Friday; nor on the other days of the week, except by special licence: which however was

[1] These were not uncommon. A good picture of such an organ, with the "divers motions in it" may be seen in Gaspar Schottius, *Magia Universalis.*
[2] Distorting mirrors?
[3] A contest in fencing.
[4] The end of the world, doomsday?
[5] "Had he lived till now, I would h' showed him at Fleet Bridge for a monster. I should have beggared the *Beginning o' th' World.*" Randolph, *Hey for Honesty* (ed. Hazlitt, p. 393).
[6] This refers, I suppose, to freak shooting.
[7] At this time "picture" was often used in the sense of "statue," "figure."

obtained by a fee paid to the Master of the Revells. (*Var.* iii. 151–153.)

"[Received] of the King's players for a *lenten dispensation*, the other companys promising to doe as muche, 44*s.* March 23, 1616.

"Of John Hemminges, in the name of the four companys,[1] for toleration in the holy-dayes, 44*s.* January 29, 1618." *Extracts from the office-book of Sir George Buc.* MSS. Herbert.

These dispensations did not extend to the sermon-days, as they were then called; that is, Wednesday and Friday in each week.[2]

After Sir Henry Herbert became possessed of the office of Master of the Revels, fees for permission to perform in Lent appear to have been constantly paid by each of the theatres. The managers however did not always perform plays during that season. Some of the theatres, particularly the Red Bull and the Fortune,[3] were then let to prize-fighters, tumblers, and rope-dancers, who sometimes added a Masque to the other exhibitions. These facts are ascertained by the following entries:

"1622. 21 Martii. For a prise[4] at the Red-Bull, for the howse;[5] the fencers would give nothing. 10*s.*" *MSS. Astley.*

"From Mr. Gunnel,[6] in the name of the dancers of the ropes, for Lent, this 15 March, 1624. £1. 0. 0."

"From Mr. Blagrave, in the name of the Cockpit company, for this Lent, this 30th March, 1624. £2. 0. 0."

"March 20, 1626. From Mr. Hemminges,[7] for this Lent allowanse, £2. 0. 0." *MSS. Herbert.* (*Var.* iii. 65–66.)

At the Restoration Herbert claimed "for Lent fee, £3"; see pp. 121, 122.

[1] See p. 62.
[2] Nor to *any* day of Holy Week.
[3] These two playhouses had a reputation for noise and vulgarity; Wright, in his *Historia Histrionica*, says that they were "most frequented by citizens and the meaner sort of people."
[4] A contest in fencing.
[5] The payment was made by the housekeepers for the privilege of opening the building.
[6] The manager of the Fortune.
[7] In behalf of the King's Company.

# VIII. PLAYS AND MASQUES AT COURT

From the time when Sir Henry Herbert came into the office of the Revels to 1642, when the theatres were shut up, his Manuscript does not furnish us with a regular account of the plays exhibited at court every year. Such, however, as he has given, I shall now subjoin,[1] together with a few anecdotes which he has preserved, relative to some of the works of our poet and the dramatick writers who immediately succeeded him. (*Var.* iii. 228.)

## I. THE SEASON 1621-2

**1621-2, Christmas.** *The Island Princess, The Pilgrim,* and *The Wild Goose Chase* are found among the court exhibitions of the year 1621. (*Var.* iii. 225-226.)[2]

## II. THE SEASON 1622-3

This [that plays were performed at court on Sundays] is ascertained by the following account of "Revels and Playes performed and acted at Christmas in the court at Whitehall, 1622;" for the preservation of which we are indebted to Sir John Astley, then Master of the Revels:

**1622, December 26.** "Upon St. Steevens daye at night *The Spanish Curate*[3] was acted by the kings players." (*Var.* iii. 146.)

**1622, December 27.** "Upon St. Johns daye at night was acted *The Beggars Bush* by the kings players." (*Var.* iii. 146.)

**1622, December 28.** "Upon Childermas daye no playe." (*Var.* iii. 146.)

**1622, December 29.** "Upon the Sonday following *The Pilgrim*[4] was acted by the kings players." (*Var.* iii. 146.)

**1622-3, January 1.** "Upon New-years day at night *The Alchemist* was acted by the kings players." (*Var.* iii. 147.)

[1] It is not to be supposed, however, that Malone gives all the notices of plays at Court which Herbert's office-book contained.
[2] Malone does not state explicitly the source of this information, but gives the impression that he secured it from Herbert's office-book, i. e. that section which was kept by Astley.
[3] By John Fletcher; licensed 1622, October 24.
[4] By John Fletcher. Fleay misdates this entry as December 30. The play was acted at Court during 1621-2; see above.

**1622–3, January 6.** "Upon Twelfe night, the Masque being put off,[1] the play called *A Vowe and a Good One*[2] was acted by the princes servants." (*Var.* iii. 147.)

**1622–3, January 19.** "Upon Sonday, being the 19th of January, the *Princes Masque* appointed for Twelfe daye, was performed.[3] The speeches and songs composed by Mr. Ben. Johnson, and the scene made by Mr. Inigo Jones, which was three tymes changed during the tyme of the masque: where in the first that was discovered was a prospective of Whitehall, with the Banqueting House; the second was the Masquers in a cloud; and the third a forrest. The French embassador was present.

"The Antemasques of tumblers and jugglers.

"The Prince did leade the measures with the French embassadors wife.

"The measures, braules, corrantos, and galliards being ended, the Masquers with the ladyes did daunce 2 contrey daunces, namely The Soldiers Marche, and Huff Hamukin, where the French Embassadors wife and Mademoysala St. Luke did [daunce]." (*Var.* iii. 147.)

**1622–3, February 2.** "At Candlemas *Malvolio*[4] was acted at court, by the kings servants." (*Var.* iii. 147.)

**1622–3, Shrovetide.** "At Shrovetide, the king being at Newmarket, and the prince out of England, there was neyther masque nor play, nor any other kind of Revells held at couıt." MS. Herbert. (*Var.* iii. 147.)

## III.   THE SEASON 1623–4

In a former page an account has been given of the court exhibitions in 1622. In Sir Henry Herbert's Office-book I find the following "Note of such playes as were acted at court in 1623 and 1624," which confirms what I have suggested, that the plays of Shakspeare were not then so much admired as those of the poets of the day. (*Var.* iii. 227.)

**1623, September 29.** "Upon Michelmas night att Hampton

[1] Jonson's *Time Vindicated;* cf. the next entry.
[2] Fleay, *B. C. E. D.* i. 200, identifies this play as Fletcher's *The Chances*, and again, *op. cit.*, ii. 98, as Middleton's *A Fair Quarrel.*
[3] See the preceding entry. The masque was Jonson's *Time Vindicated*, which in the Dulwich College MS. is called *The Prince's Masque.*
[4] Shakespeare's *Twelfth Night.*

court, *The Mayd of the Mill*,[1] by the K. company." (*Var.* iii. 227.)

**1623, November 1.** "Upon Allhollows night at St. James, the prince being there only, *The Mayd of the Mill* againe, with reformations." (*Var.* iii. 227.)

**1623, November 5.** "Upon the fifth of November att Whitehall, the prince being there only, *The Gipsye*,[2] by the Cockpitt company." (*Var.* iii. 227.)

**1623, December 26.** "Upon St. Stevens daye, the king and prince being there, *The Mayd of the Mill*,[3] by the K. company Att Whitehall." (*Var.* iii. 227.)

**1623, December 27.** "Upon St. John's night, the prince only being there, *The Bondman*,[4] by the queene [of Bohemia's] company. Att Whitehall." (*Var.* iii. 227.)

**1623, December 28.** "Upon Innocents night, falling out upon a Sonday, *The Buck is a Thief*,[5] the king and prince being there. By the king's company. At Whitehall." (*Var.* iii. 227.)

**1623-4, January 1.** "Upon New-years night, by the K. company, *The Wandering Lovers*,[6] the prince only being there. Att Whitehall." (*Var.* iii. 227.)

**1623-4, January 4.** "Upon the Sonday after, beinge the 4 of January 1623, by the Queene of Bohemias company, *The Change-linge*, the prince only being there. Att Whitehall." (*Var.* iii. 227.)

**1623-4, January 6.** "Upon Twelfe Night, the maske being put off,[7] *More Dissemblers besides Women*,[8] by the king's company, the prince only being there. Att Whitehall." (*Var.* iii. 227.)

**1623-4, January 18.** "To the Duchess of Richmond, in the kings absence, was given *The Winter's Tale*,[9] by the K. company, the 18 Janu. 1623. Att Whitehall." (*Var.* iii. 228.)

---

[1] *The Maid in the Mill*, licensed 1623, August 29, as written by Fletcher and Rowley. It was again acted at Court on November 1 and December 26.
[2] *The Spanish Gipsy*, by Middleton and Rowley.
[3] Acted for the third time; see September 29 and November 1.
[4] *The Noble Bondman*, by Massinger, licensed 1623, December 3.
[5] Not extant. Fleay, *B. C. E. D.* i. 218, suggests that it is the same as *Wit at Several Weapons*, and again, *op. cit.*, i. 197, *The Devil of Dowgate*.
[6] Licensed 1623, December 6, as by John Fletcher. For a discussion of the play see the note to the license entry, page 27.
[7] Ben Jonson's *Neptune's Triumph*.
[8] By Thomas Middleton, licensed 1623, October 17. In the margin, says Malone, Herbert has written: "The worst play that ere I saw."
[9] The play was licensed by Herbert for a revival, 1623, August 19.

## IV.  THE SEASON 1624-5

**1624, November 1.**  "Upon All-hollows night, 1624, the king beinge at Roiston, no play."  (*Var.* iii. 228.)

**1624, November 2.**  "The night after, my Lord Chamberlin had *Rule a Wife and Have a Wife*[1] for the ladys, by the kings company."  (*Var.* iii. 228.)

**1624, December 26.**  "Upon St. Steevens night, the prince only being there, [was acted] *Rule a Wife and Have a Wife*, by the kings company.  Att Whitehall."[2]  (*Var.* iii. 228.)

**1624, December 27.**  "Upon St. John's night, [the prince] and the duke of Brunswick being there, *The Fox*, by the ————.[3] At Whitehall."  (*Var.* iii. 228.)

**1624, December 28.**  "Upon Innocents night, the [prince] and the duke of Brunswyck being there, *Cupids Revenge*, by the Queen of Bohemia's Servants.[4]  Att Whitehall, 1624."  (*Var.* iii. 228.)

**1624-5, January 1.**  "Upon New-years night, the prince only being there, *The First Part of Sir John Falstaff*,[5] by the kings company.  Att Whitehall, 1624."  (*Var.* iii. 228.)

**1624-5, January 6.**  "Upon Twelve night, the Masque[6] being putt of, and the prince only there, *Tu Quoque*, by the Queene of Bohemias servants.  Att Whitehall, 1624."  (*Var.* iii. 228.)

**1624-5, January 9.**  "Upon the Sonday night following, being the ninthe of January 1624, the Masque was performd."[7] (*Var.* iii. 228.)

**1624-5, February 2.**  "On Candlemas night the 2 February, no play, the king being att Newmarket."  (*Var.* iii. 228.)

---

[1] By John Fletcher, licensed 1624, October 19.  It was performed at Court a second time on December 26; see the following entry.

[2] See the preceding entry.

[3] Apparently this entry shows some of the mouldering away spoken of by Malone.  *The Fox* belonged to the King's Company.

[4] Fleay, *History of the Stage*, p. 258, incorrectly states that the play was acted by the King's Men.  It was again acted at Court on February 7, 1636-7.

[5] Shakespeare's *Henry IV*, Part I.

[6] Ben Jonson's *The Fortunate Isles*.

[7] Ben Jonson's *The Fortunate Isles;* see the preceding entry.  Fleay, *History of the Stage*, p. 262, says: "Neptune's Triumph, with the addition of the Fortunate Isles and their Union"; and quotes the Herbert MS. as stating: "the Prince only being there."  This, of course, is an error arising from the preceding entry.

## V. THE SEASON 1633-4

**1633, November 16.** "On Saterday, the 17th of Novemb. being the Queens birthday,[1] *Richarde the Thirde* was acted by the K. players at St. James, wher the king and queene were present, it being the first play the queene sawe since her M.ᵉˢ delivery of the Duke of York, 1633." (*Var.* iii. 233 234.)

**1633, November 19.** "On tusday, the 19th of November, being the king's birth-day, *The Yong Admirall*[2] was acted at St. James by the queen's players, and likt by the K. and Queen." (*Var.* iii. 234.)

**1633, November 26.** "On tusday night at Saint James, the 26th of Novemb. 1633, was acted before the King and Queene, *The Taminge of the Shrew.* Likt." (*Var.* iii. 234.)

**1633, November 28.** "On thursday night at St. James, the 28 of Novemb. 1633, was acted before the King and Queene, *The Tamer Tamd*, made by Fletcher. Very well likt."[3] (*Var.* iii. 234.)

**1633, December 10.** "On tusday night at Whitehall the 10 of Decemb. 1633, was acted before the King and Queen, *The Loyal Subject*,[4] made by Fletcher, and very well likt by the king." (*Var.* iii. 234.)

**1633, December 16.** "On Monday night the 16 of December, 1633, at Whitehall was acted before the King and Queen, *Hymens Holliday or Cupids Fegarys*,[5] an ould play of Rowleys. Likte." (*Var.* iii. 234.)

**1633-4, January 1.** "On Wensday night the first of January, 1633, *Cymbeline* was acted at court by the Kings players. Well likte by the kinge." (*Var.* iii. 234.)

**1633-4, January 6.** "On Monday night, the sixth of January and the Twelfe Night, was presented at Denmark-house, before the King and Queene, Fletchers pastorall called *The Faithfull Shepheardesse*, in the clothes the Queene had given Taylor the year before of her owne pastorall.[6]

[1] As Fleay points out, the date should be Saturday the 16th of November.
[2] By James Shirley, licensed 1633, July 3. For Herbert's comments on the play see page 19.
[3] On October 18, 1633, Herbert suppressed the play, on October 21 he returned the MS. "purgd of oaths." See page 20.
[4] It was originally licensed by Sir George Buc, November 16, 1618, and relicensed by Herbert, with reformations, November 23, 1633.
[5] Licensed 1633, August 15: see the note to that entry.
[6] *The Queen's Pastoral*, by W. Montague, performed at Denmark House in January, 1632-3.

"The scenes were fitted to the pastorall, and made, by Mr. Inigo Jones, in the great chamber, 1633." (*Var.* iii. 234–235.)

**1633–4, January 12.**  "*The Guardian,*[1] a play of Mr. Messengers, was acted at court on Sunday the 12 January, 1633, by the Kings players, and well likte." (*Var.* iii. 235.)

**1633–4, January 14.**  "*The Tale of the Tub*[2] was acted on tusday night at Court, the 14 Janua. 1633, by the Queenes players, and not likte." (*Var.* iii. 236.)

**1633–4, January 16.**  "*The Winters Tale* was acted on thursday night at Court, the 16 Janua. 1633, by the K. players, and likt." (*Var.* iii. 236.)

**1633–4, January 28.**  "*The Witts*[3] was acted on tusday night the 28 January, 1633, at Court, before the Kinge and Queene. Well likt. It had a various fate on the stage, and at court, though the kinge commended the language, but dislikt the plott and characters." (*Var.* iii. 236.)

**1633–4, January 30.**  "*The Night-Walkers*[4] was acted on thursday night the 30 Janua. 1633, at Court, before the King and Queen. Likt as a merry play. Made by Fletcher." (*Var.* iii. 236.)

**1633–4, February 3.**  "The Inns of court gentlemen presented their masque[5] at court, before the kinge and queene, the 2 February, 1633, and performed it very well.[6] Their shew through the streets was glorious, and in the nature of a triumph. —Mr. Surveyor Jones invented and made the scene;[7] Mr. Sherley the poett made the prose and verse." (*Var.* iii. 236.)

**1633–4, February 6.**  "On thursday night the 6 of Febru. 1633, *The Gamester* was acted at Court, made by Sherley, out of a plot of the king's, given him by mee;[8] and well likte. The

---

[1] Licensed 1633, October 31.

[2] Licensed 1633, May 7.

[3] Licensed 1633–4, January 19. For Herbert's censorship of the play, and the King's interference, see page 22.

[4] Licensed 1633, May 11.

[5] *The Triumph of Peace*, published in 1633 as "A Masque presented by the Foure Honourable Houses, or Innes of Court. Before the King and Queens Majesties, in the Banqueting House at White Hall, February the third, 1633." See also the Privy Council Register, January 29, 1633–4.

[6] It was so well liked that at the King's command it was repeated on February 11 in the Merchant Tailors' Hall.

[7] For a reproduction of Jones's design for the scene see W. J. Lawrence, *The Elizabethan Playhouse*, p. 101.

[8] Gerard Langbaine, p. 479, says that the plot was taken from Malespini's *Ducento Novelle*, Part ii. Nov. 96, or Queen Margaret's Novels i. 8.

king sayd it was the best play he had seen for seven years."
(*Var.* iii. 236.)

**1633-4, February 18.** "On Shrovetusday night, the 18 of
February, 1633, the Kinge dancte his Masque,[1] accompanied
with 11 lords, and attended with 10 pages. It was the noblest
masque of my time to this day, the best poetrye, best scenes,
and the best habitts. The kinge and queene were very well
pleasd with my service, and the Q. was pleasd to tell mee before
the king, 'Pour les habits, elle n'avoit jamais rien vue de si
brave.'"    (*Var.* iii. 236-237.)

**1634, April 7.** "*Bussy d'Amboise* was playd by the king's
players on Easter-monday night, at the Cockpitt in court."[2]
(*Var.* iii. 237.)

**1634, April 8.** "The Pastorall[3] was playd by the king's
players on Easter-tusday night, at the Cockpitt in court."
(*Var.* iii. 237.)

## VI.  THE SEASON 1635-6

**1635, December 21.** "Le pastorale de *Florimene*[4] fust repre-
senté devant le roy et la royne, le prince Charles, et le prince
Palatin, le 21 Decem. jour de St. Thomas, par les filles Françoise
de la royne, et firent tres bien, dans la grande sale de Whitehall,
aux depens de la royne."  MS. Herbert.  (*Var.* iii. 122.)

**1635-6, February 16.** "The Second part of *Arviragus and
Philicia*[5] playd at court the 16 Febru. 1635, with great approbation of K. and Queene."  (*Var.* iii. 237.)

**1635-6, February 18.** "*The Silent Woman* playd at Court of
St. James on thursday ye 18 Febr. 1635."  (*Var.* iii. 237.)

[1] Thomas Carew's *Cœlum Britannicum*.
[2] This was a small theatre-royal attached to that section of Whitehall
Palace known as The Cockpit.
[3] Probably "Fletcher's pastorall, called *The Faithful Shepherdess*," which
had been presented at Court on January 6, 1633-4. Since, however, *The
Pastorall* immediately followed Chapman's *Bussy d'Amboise*, we may wonder
whether it could be Chapman's "pastorall tragedie," or "a Pastorall ending
in a Tragedye," written for Henslowe in 1599 and now lost.
[4] The author of the masque is unknown. It was in French, hence Herbert's
entry in French. Lord Herbert of Cherbury tells us that "Henry, after he
had been brought up in learning, as the other brothers were, was sent by his
friends into France, where he attained the language of that country in much
perfection." The plan of the scenes for the masque, drawn by Inigo Jones,
has been reproduced by P. Reyher, *Les Masques Anglais*, p. 346, and by
W. J. Lawrence, *The Elizabethan Playhouse*, p. 48. On December 21, 1635,
"the argument only, put into English" was licensed by Herbert to be printed,
see p. 41.
[5] By Lodowick Carlell. Both parts were acted at Court on April 18 and
19, 1636, and on December 26 and 27, 1636.

**1635–6, February 22.** "*The Dukes Mistres*[1] played at St. James the 22 of Feb. 1635.    Made by Sherley." (*Var.* iii. 238.)

**1635–6, February 23.** "On Wensday the 23 of Febru. 1635, the Prince d'Amours gave a masque[2] to the Prince Elector and his brother, in the Middle Temple, wher the Queene was pleasd to grace the entertaynment by putting of [off] majesty to putt on a citizens habitt, and to sett upon the scaffold on the right hande amongst her subjects.

"The queene was attended in the like habitts by the Marques Hamilton, the Countess of Denbighe, the Countess of Holland, and the Lady Elizabeth Feildinge.    Mrs. Basse, the law-woman, leade in this royal citizen and her company.

"The Earle of Holland, the Lord Goringe, Mr. Percy, and Mr. Jermyn, were the men that attended.

"The Prince Elector satt in the midst, his brother Robert on the right hand of him, and the Prince d'Amours on the left.

"The Masque was very well performed in the dances, scenes, cloathinge, and musique, and the Queene was pleasd to tell mee at her going away, that she liked it very well.

"Henry Lause   ⎫
"William Lause ⎬ made the musique.
            ⎭

"Mr. Corseilles made the scenes." (*Var.* iii. 237–238.)

**1635–6, February 24.** "*Loves Aftergame*,[3] played at St. James by the Salisbury Court players, the 24 of Feb. 1635." (*Var.* iii. 238.)

**1635–36, February 25.** [See the note to the entry above, February 22.]

**1635–6, February 28.** "The 28 Feb. *The Knight of the Burning Pestle*, playd by the Q. men at St. James." (*Var.* iii. 238.)

**1636, April 18, 19.** "The first and second part of *Arviragus and Philicia*[4] were acted at the Cockpitt, [Whitehall] before the Kinge and Queene, the Prince, and Prince Elector, the 18 and 19 Aprill, 1636, being monday and tusday in Easter weeke." [5] (*Var.* iii. 238.)

---

[1] Licensed January 18, 1635–6.  Since Herbert is giving a continuous account of Court performances in chronological order, and since this entry follows the entry of February 24 and precedes the entry of February 28, I believe that the correct date is February 25.  The numerals 2 and 5 may have been confused by the transcriber or the printer.

[2] *The Triumphs of the Prince d'Amour*, by William Davenant.

[3] Not extant.  Licensed 1634, November 24.

[4] The Second Part had been acted at Court on February 16, 1635–6, and both parts were repeated on December 26 and 27, 1636.

[5] See p. 75.

## VII. THE SEASON 1636-7

### "At Hampton Court, 1636." [1]

**1636, December 26.** "The first part of *Arviragus*, Monday Afternoon, 26 Decemb."

**1636, December 27.** "The second part of *Arviragus*, tusday 27 Decemb."[2]

**1636-7, January 1.** "*Love and Honour*, on New-years night, sonday." [3]

**1636-7, January 5.** "*The Elder Brother*, on thursday the 5 Janua." [4]

**1636-7, January 10.** "*The Kinge and no Kinge*, on tusday y° 10 Janua." [5]

**1636-7, January 12.** "*The Royal Slave*, on thursday the 12 of Janu.[6]—Oxford play, written by Cartwright.[7] The king gave him forty pounds." [8]

**1636-7, January 24.** "*Rollo*, the 24 Janu." [9]

**1636-7, January 31.** "*Julius Caesar*, at St. James, the 31 Janu. 1636." [10]

**1636-7, February 7.** "*Cupides Revenge*, at St. James, by Beeston's boyes, the 7 Febru." [11]

[1] Because of the plague in London the theatres had been closed, and the royal family had secluded itself at Hampton Court. The King's company of players, however, was ordered by the King "to assemble their companie and keepe themselves togither neere our Court for our service." This explains the large number of plays acted at Hampton. For other plays not here noted see pp. 75-76.

[2] See ante, February 16, 1635-6, April 18 and 19, 1636. And see p. 76.

[3] See p. 76. The play was licensed 1634, November 20.

[4] See p. 76. See also under the license entry 1634-5, January 10.

[5] See p. 76.

[6] See p. 76.

[7] The play had been acted before the King and Queen at Oxford on August 30, 1636.

[8] Chalmers, *Apology*, pp. 507-508, says: "The acting of Cartwright's *Royal Slave*, on Thursday the 12th of January 1636-7, before the King at Hampton-court, cost one hundred and fifty-four pounds, exclusive of forty pounds, which Sir Henry Herbert says the King gave the author." The former sum, £154, was paid by the Lord Chamberlain on April 4, 1637, for "ye alterations, reparations, and additions which were made unto ye scene, apparell, and properties." And on March 16, the Chamberlain paid to the King's Men £30 "for the new play called the Royall Slave." See Mrs. Stopes, in the Shakespeare *Jahrbuch*, xlvi. 99.

[9] The actors dated this performance January 17, and stated that they acted *Hamlet* on January 24; see p. 76.

[10] See p. 76.

[11] It was acted at Court on December 28, 1624, and several times previous to that date.

**1636–7, February 9.** "*A Wife for a Monthe*, by the K. players, at St. James, the 9 Febru." [1]

**1636–7, February 14.** "*Wit without Money*, by the B. boyes[2] at St. James, the 14 Feb."

**1636–7, February 17.** "*The Governor*, by the K. players, at St. James, the 17 Febru. 1636." [3]

**1636–7, February 21.** "*Philaster*, by the K. players, at St. James, shrovtusday, the 21 Febru. 1636." [4]   (*Var.* iii. 239.)

## VIII. THE SEASONS 1638–1642

**1638, March 26–January 7, 1639.** [For the Court plays acted by the King's Company during this period, see pp. 76–77.]

**1640, April 9.** "On thursday the 9 of Aprill, 1640, my Lord Chamberlen bestow'd a play on the Kinge and Queene, call'd *Cleodora, Queene of Arragon*, made by my cozen Abington.[5] It was performd by my lords servants out of his own family, and his charge in the cloathes and sceanes, which were very riche and curious.   In the hall at Whitehall.

"The king and queen commended the generall entertaynment, as very well acted, and well set out.

"It was acted the second tyme in the same place before the king and queene." (*Var.* iii. 240–241.)

**1641–2, January 6.** "On Twelfe Night, 1641, the prince had a play called *The Scornful Lady*, at the Cockpitt, but the kinge and queene were not there; and it was the only play acted at courte in the whole Christmas." (*Var.* iii. 241.)

---

[1] See p. 76.   The play was licensed 1624, May 27.
[2] The King and Queen's Company, popularly known as Beeston's Boys; see p. 66.
[3] The actors dated this performance February 16; see p. 76.   A play called *The Governor*, by Sir Cornelius Formido, was entered S. R., September 9, 1653, but not printed.   In Warburton's list we find "The Governor T. Sʳ. Corñ. Fermido."   Fleay, *B. C. E. D.* i. 235, says: "The MS. was destroyed by Warburton's cook"; but it is safe in the British Museum (Add. MSS. 10,419), with the inscription: "This play formerly belonged to John Warburton, Somerset Herald."
[4] See p. 76.
[5] William Habington.   The play was presented at Blackfriars, and was printed in 1640 with the title *The Queene of Arragon*.

## IX.  THE FRENCH PLAYERS OF 1629

The visit of a troupe of French actors to London in the autumn of 1629 created something of a sensation, mainly, it seems, because it gave the English their first opportunity to see women on the public stage.  Thomas Brande writes on November 8, 1629:[1]

> Furthermore you should know that last daye certaine vagrant French players, who had beene expelled from their owne contrey, and those women did attempt, thereby giving just offence to all vertuous and well-disposed persons in this town, to act a certain lascivious and unchaste comedye in the French tonge at the Blackfryers.  Glad I am to saye they were hissed, hooted, and pippen-pelted from the stage, so as I do not thinke they will soone be ready to try the same againe.—Whether they had license for so doing I know not; but I do know that if they had license it were fit that the Master [of the Revels] be called to account for the same.

Prynne writes: "Some French-women, or monsters, rather, in Michaelmas term, 1629, attempted to act a French play at the playhouse in Blackfriars, an impudent, shameful, unwomanish, graceless, if not more than whorish attempt"; yet he adds: "to which there was great resort."

Below are the Herbert entries regarding these players:

"For the allowinge of a French company to playe a farse at Blackfryers, this 4 of November, 1629,—2*l*. 0*s*. 0*d*."[2]  (*Var.* iii. 120.)

"For allowinge of the Frenche [company] at the Red Bull for a daye, 22 Novemb. 1629,—[2*l*. 0*s*. 0*d*.]."  (*Var.* iii. 120.)

"For allowinge of a Frenche companie att the Fortune to play one afternoone, this 14 Day of Decemb. 1629.— 1*l*. 0*s*. 0*d*.

---

[1] Printed by Collier, *A History of English Dramatic Poetry* (1879), i. 452. The year is not given, but can be readily ascertained from Herbert's office book.

[2] By an error the Variorum prints "1639" for "1629", the 1790 Malone gives the date correctly.

"I should have had another peece, but in respect of their ill fortune, I was content to bestow a peece back." MS. Herbert. (*Var.* iii. 120.)


## X. THE FRENCH PLAYERS OF 1635

In February, 1635, some distinguished French players, under the leadership of Josias de Soulas, better known by his stage name of Floridor,[1] visited London, and won such favor at the Court that they were permitted to use the Cockpit Playhouse in Drury Lane during Lent, and afterwards to fit up for themselves a temporary theatre in a riding school in Drury Lane. The history of these players is mainly found in the records of Herbert and of the Lord Chamberlain. From the former Malone has preserved the following entries:

"On tuesday night the 17 of February, 1634, [1634-5,] a Frenche company of players, being approved of by the queene at her house[2] too nights before, and commended by her majesty to the kinge, were admitted to the Cockpitt in Whitehall,[3] and there presented the king and queene with a Frenche comedy called *Melise*,[4] with good approbation: for which play the king gives them ten pounds.[5]

"This day being Friday, and the 20 of the same monthe, the kinge tould mee his pleasure, and commanded mee to give order that this Frenche company should playe the too sermon daies in the weeke, during their time of playinge in Lent,[6] and

---

[1] See Frederick Hawkins, *Annals of the French Stage*, 1884, i. 148 ff. for the career of this player on the French stage. "Every gift required by the actor," says Hawkins, "was possessed by Floridor."

[2] Denmark House. Queen Henrietta Maria, it should be remembered, was a French princess, and her house was filled with many French servants and followers.

[3] The little theatre-royal attached to the palace at Whitehall; to be carefully distinguished from the Cockpit in Drury Lane.

[4] *La Melise, ou les Princes Reconnus*, by Du Rocher, first acted in Paris in 1633; see *The Athenæum*, July 11, 1891, p. 73.

[5] This was the sum regularly given by the king for performances in the Cockpit.

[6] I. e. Wednesdays and Fridays, on which days during Lent the English actors were never allowed to play.

in the house of Drury-lane, where the queenes players usually playe.[1]

"The kings pleasure I signifyed to Mr. Beeston, [the Manager of Drury-lane theatre,] the same day, who obeyd readily.

"The house-keepers are to give them by promise the benefit of their interest for the two days of the first weeke.[2]

"They had the benefitt of playinge on the sermon daies, and gott two hundred pounds at least; besides many rich clothes were given them.

"They had freely to themselves the whole weeke before the weeke before Easter, which I obtaynd of the king for them.[3]

"The 4 April, on Easter monday,[4] they playd the *Trompeur puny*,[5] with better approbation than the other.[6]

"On Wensday night the 16 Aprill, 1635,[7] the French playd *Alcimedor*[8] with good approbation."

In a marginal note Sir Henry Herbert adds, "The Frenche offered mee a present of 10*l*.; but I refused itt, and did them many other curtesys, *gratis*, to render the queene my mistris an acceptable service." (*Var.* iii. 121.)

"A warrant granted to Josias D'Aunay,[9] Hurfries de Lau, and others, for to act playes at a new house in Drury-lane, during pleasure, y° 5 may, 1635.[10]

[1] The Cockpit Playhouse.
[2] The "house-keepers" were the proprietors of the building as distinguished from the actors. They always demanded of the players as rental for the building a certain share of each day's takings. Herbert simply means that the proprietors of the Cockpit promised to allow the French company to use the playhouse without paying anything therefor for the first two days; after that, presumably, the proprietors demanded their customary share of the takings.
[3] That is, Passion Week, during which time the English companies were never allowed to act.
[4] This must be an error, for in 1635 Easter Monday fell on March 30. Herbert seems to be writing from memory.
[5] *Le Trompeur Puni, ou Histoire Septentrionale*, by Scuderi.
[6] The place is not stated; but the use of the Cockpit in Drury Lane doubtless came to an end at Easter, after which time Beeston's company of English actors would require the playhouse for themselves. We may safely infer, I think, that the French players acted at the Cockpit at Whitehall.
[7] Wednesday was the fifteenth.
[8] *Alcimedon*, by Duryer.
[9] Was this his real name, or is there an error in the transcript? Elsewhere he is referred to as Josias Floridor, and his real name is supposed to have been Josias de Soulas. Possibly we should insert a comma after "Josias."
[10] This was made necessary by the fact that with the passing of Lent the French players were driven out of the Cockpit Playhouse in Drury Lane. The King thereupon gave them permission to convert the riding school of M. Le Febure in Drury Lane into a temporary theatre, as explained in the next sentence.

"The king was pleased to commande my Lord Chamberlain to direct his warrant to Monsieur Le Fevure, to give him a power to contract with the Frenchemen for to builde a playhouse in the manage-house, which was done accordinglye by my advise and allowance." [1] (*Var.* iii. 122.)

"Thes Frenchmen," Sir Henry adds in the margin, "were commended unto mee by the queene, and have passed through my handes, *gratis.*"

They did not, however, pass quite free, for from a subsequent entry it appears, that "they gave Blagrave [Sir Henry's deputy] three pounds for his paines." [2] (*Var.* iii. 122.)

## XI. MISCELLANEOUS

When the sceptre of the stage was delivered into his hands, there appears from the record of his office to have been four established companies of players;[3] exclusive of strangers,[4] who sometimes invaded their territories. (*S. A.* 211.)

Soon after· his [Shakespeare's] death, four of the principal companies then subsisting, made a union, and were afterwards called The United Companies; but I know not precisely in what this union consisted. (*Var.* iii. 224.)

It appears from the office-book of Sir Henry Herbert, Master of the Revels to King James the First, and the two succeeding kings, that very soon after our poet's [Shakespeare's] death, in

---

[1] In the Lord Chamberlain's office-book we find: "18 April 1635: His Majesty hath commanded me to signify his royal pleasure that the French comedians (having agreed with Mons. le Febure) may erect a stage, scaffolds, and seats, and all other accommodations which shall be convenient, and act and present interludes and stage plays at his house [the manage-house, or riding-school] in Drury Lane, during His Majesty's pleasure, without any disturbance, hindrance, or interruption. And this shall be to them, and Mr. le Febure, and to all others, a sufficient discharge, &c."

[2] How long the French players occupied their temporary playhouse in Drury Lane is not clear. In the Lord Chamberlain's book we find an entry which shows that they presented a play at Court in December 1635: "Warrant to pay £10 to Josias Floridor for himself and the rest of the French players for a tragedy by them played before His Majesty Dec. last." The entry is dated January 8, 1635–6, and so far as I can discover, this is the last reference to the French players in London. We may suppose that shortly after this they returned to Paris.

[3] See p. 65: "On the 12th of May, 1636, warrants were sent to the *four* companies to stop the plays, on account of the pest"; p. 48: "Of John Hemminges, in the name of the four companys, for toleration in the holy-days, 44s. January 29, 1618."; and p. 25: "they were none of the four companies."

[4] See pp. 25, 26, 63.

the year 1622, there were but five principal companies of comedians in London; the King's Servants, who performed at the Globe and in Blackfriars; the Prince's Servants, who performed then at the Curtain; the Palsgrave's Servants, who had possession of the Fortune; the players of the Revels, who acted at the Red Bull; and the Lady Elizabeth's Servants, or, as they are sometimes denominated, the Queen of Bohemia's players, who performed at the Cockpit in Drury Lane. (*Var.* iii. 57 59.)

"1622. The Palsgrave's servants. Frank Grace, Charles Massy, Richard Price, Richard Fowler, - - Kane,[1] Curtys Grevill." MS. Herbert. Three other names have perished. Of these one must have been that of Richard Gunnel, who was then the manager of the Fortune theatre; and another, that of William Cartwright, who was of the same company.

"The names of the chiefe players at the Red Bull, called the players of the Revells. Robert Lee, Richard Perkings, Ellis Woorth, Thomas Basse, John Blany, John Cumber, William Robbins." *Ibidem.*

"The chiefe of them at the Phoenix. Christopher Beeston, Joseph More, Eliard Swanson, Andrew Cane, Curtis Grevill, William Shurlock, Anthony Turner." *Ibidem.* Eliard Swanston in 1624 joined the company at Blackfriars.

That part of the leaf which contained the list of the king's servants, and the performers at the *Curtain* is mouldered away. (*Var.* iii. 59-60.)

We have already seen[2] that John Heminges in 1618 pay'd Sir George Buck, "in the name of the four companys, for a lenten dispensation in the holydaies, 44s.;" and Sir Henry Herbert observes that the play called *Come See a Wonder,*[3] "written by John Daye for a company of strangers," and represented Sept. 18, 1623, was "acted at the Red Bull, and licensed without his hand to it, because they [i. e. this company of strangers] were none of the *four* companys." (*Var.* iii. 224.)

After the year 1620, as appears from Sir Henry Herbert's office-book, they [the Swan and the Rose playhouses] were used occasionally for the exhibition of prize-fighters.[4] (*Var.* iii. 56

[1] Andrew Cane. The name of Cane and Grevill are repeated below in the list of "The chiefe of them at the Phoenix." For a discussion of this fact see Murray, *English Dramatic Companies,* i. 215 216.

[2] *Var.* iii. 65; see p. 48.

[3] Fleay identifies this with *The Wonder of a Kingdom.*

[4] This may have been true of the Swan, but Malone is surely mistaken as to the Rose, for that playhouse was torn down or converted into tenements before April 25, 1606, when it is referred to as "the late playhouse." see Adams, *Shakespearean Playhouses,* p. 160.

It appears from Sir Henry Herbert's Official Register, that on the 1st of July, 1625, he granted a Confirmation of the King's Company's Patent *to travel, for a year.* [Rym. Foed. 18 T. p. 120.]   (*S. A.* 185.)

"17 July, 1626, [Received] from Mr. Hemmings for a courtesie done him about their Blackfriers hous,—3*l.* o. o."   (*Var.* iii. 229.)

"[Received] from Mr. Hemming, in their company's name, to forbid the playing of Shakespeare's plays,[1] to the Red Bull Company, this 11 of April, 1627,—5*l.* o. o."   (*Var.* iii. 229.)

I suspect he [John Heminges] died of the plague, which had raged so violently that year [1630], that the playhouses were shut up in April,[2] and not permitted to be opened till the 12th of November, at which time the weekly bill of those who died in London of that distemper, was diminished to twenty-nine. MS. Herbert.   (*Var.* iii. 190–191.)

"Received of Mr. Benfielde, in the name of the kings company, for a gratuity for ther liberty gaind unto them of playinge, upon the cessation of the plague, this 10 of June, 1631,—3*l.* 10*s.* 0*d.*"—"This (Sir Henry Herbert adds) was taken upon *Pericles* at the Globe."[3]   (*Var.* iii. 177.)

"I committed Cromes, a broker in Longe Lane, the 16 of Febru. 1634, to the Marshalsey, for lending a church-robe with the name of JESUS upon it, to the players in Salisbury Court, to present a Flamen, a priest of the heathens.[4]   Upon his petition of submission, and acknowledgment of his faulte, I releasd him, the 17 Febru. 1634."   (*Var.* iii. 237.)

[1] At this time Shakespeare's plays were readily available in the First Folio, 1623.   On August 10, 1639, the Lord Chamberlain issued an order that no other company of actors should perform the plays belonging to the Cockpit Company (see Mrs. Stopes's extracts from the Lord Chamberlain's office-book, Shakespeare *Jahrbuch*, xlvi. 101); more interesting, however, is a similar order issued to the King's Men in 1641 (see the Malone Society's *Collections*, i. 364).   Of interest in this connection, also, is the letter from Mosely printed on p. 90.

[2] From the office-book of the Lord Chamberlain we learn that the warrant for suppressing plays was issued on April 17, 1630.

[3] Apparently the actors gave a benefit performance for Herbert.

[4] Compare the following letter of Edmond Rossingham, dated May 8, 1639 (in *The Calendar of State Papers, Domestic Series, 1639*, p. 140): "Thursday last the players of the Fortune were fined £1,000 for setting up an altar, a bason, and two candlesticks, and bowing down before it upon the stage; and although they allege it was an old play revived, and an altar to the heathen gods, yet it was apparent that this play was revived on purpose in contempt of the ceremonies of the Church."

"The 13 May, 1634, the Queene was at Blackfriars[1] to see Messengers playe."[2] (*Var.* iii. 167.)

"At the increase of the plague to 4 within the citty[3] and 54 in all.—This day the 12 May, 1636,[4] I received a warrant from my lord Chamberlin for the suppressing of playes and shews, and at the same time delivered my severall warrants to George Wilson for the four companys of players,[5] to be served upon them." (*Var.* iii. 239.)

On the 12th of May, 1636, warrants were sent to the *four* companies to stop the plays, on account of the pest. Owing to the same cause, Sir Henry, upon conference with the Earl of Essex, the Lord Chamberlain,[6] concerning the plague, which had increased to a hundred deaths a week, sent warrants, by Mr. Louens, on the 5th of August, to the several playhouses, for the purpose of preventing their representations: The plague, having decreased to eighty-six deaths a week, induced the Lord Chamberlain to open the theatres, for the profit of the players, and the amusement of the people. (*S. A.* 211-212.)

"On thursday morning the 23 of February the bill of the plague made the number at forty foure,[7] upon which decrease the king gave the players their liberty, and they began the 24 February 1636. [1636–7.]

"The plague encreasinge,[8] the players laye still[9] untill the 2 of October, when they had leave to play.

[1] Since Herbert makes no comment on this visit we may suppose that it was not unusual. Scholars have assumed that the Queen attended a regular afternoon performance, but evidence shows that on occasions the actors made use of the playhouse at night for entertaining members of the royal family and their invited guests; see Adams, *Shakespearean Playhouses*, p. 232-33.

[2] Malone adds: "The play which her majesty honoured with her presence was *The Tragedy of Cleander*, which had been produced on the 7th of the same month."

[3] There must be an error here. For "4" read "41," says Fleay.

[4] Privy Council Records, May 10, 1636: "Ordered that the Lord Chamberlain of the Queen's Majestie's household should be hereby prayed and required to cause the players . . . to forbear all stage plays."

[5] See p. 62.

[6] The Earl of Essex was not then the Lord Chamberlain; he "received the staff" on "Julie 24. 1641." Does Chalmers mean "The Earl of Essex and the Lord Chamberlain"?

[7] Fleay, *History of the Stage*, p. 340, says that the Mortality Bill gives 33 as the correct number.

[8] On March 1 the number of deaths had risen to 57.

[9] See Privy Council Records, March 1, 1636-7, for the "Warrant to suppress all plays."

"Mr. Beeston was commanded to make a company of boyes,[1] and began to play at the Cockpit with them the same day.[2]

"I disposed of Perkins, Sumner, Sherlock and Turner, to Salisbury Court, and joynd them with the best of that company." [3]   (*Var.* iii. 239–240.)

"At Easter 1640, the Princes company went to the Fortune, and the Fortune company to the Red Bull."   (*Var.* iii. 241.)

"On Monday the 4 May, 1640, William Beeston[4] was taken by a messenger, and committed to the Marshalsey, by my Lord Chamberlens warant, for playinge a playe without license.  The same day the company at the Cockpitt was commanded by my Lord Chamberlens warant to forbeare playinge, for playinge when they were forbidden by mee, and for other disobedience, and laye still monday, tusday, and wensday.  On thursday at my Lord Chamberlen's entreaty I gave them their liberty, and upon their petition of submission subscribed by the players, I restored them to their liberty on thursday.

"The play I cald for, and, forbiddinge the playinge of it, keepe the booke, because it had relation to the passages of the K.s journey into the Northe, and was complaynd of by his M.$^{tye}$ to mee, with commande to punishe the offenders."   (*Var.* iii. 241.)

It appears from Sir Henry Herbert's Office-book that the king's company between the years 1622 and 1641 produced either at Blackfriars or the Globe at least four new plays every year.   (*Var.* iii. 166.)

It appears from Sir Henry Herbert's Manuscript, that the

---

[1] In the office-book of the Lord Chamberlain, under the date February 21, 1636–7, we find: "Warrant to swear Mr. Christopher Beeston His Majesty's Servant in the place of Governor of the new company of the King's and Queen's Boys."  The new company was popularly known as Beeston's Boys.

[2] Presumably October 2.  Their first recorded performance was at Court on February 7, 1637, and on May 10 Beeston was paid for "two plays acted by the New Company"; see Adams, *Shakespearean Playhouses*, p. 357.

[3] These four actors were the chief members of Beeston's old company at the Cockpit, Queen Henrietta's Men.  At Salisbury Court they joined the Queen's new Company.

[4] Who in 1639 had succeeded his father, Christopher Beeston, as Governor of the King and Queen's company, at the Cockpit in Drury Lane.  Malone, *Var.* iii. 242, wrongly supposes that Sir William Davenant succeeded Christopher Beeston; "and I suppose he appointed her son Mr. William Beeston his deputy, for from Sir Henry Herbert's office-book, he appears for a short time to have had the management of that theatre."  Davenant was appointed Governor of the Cockpit company after William Beeston was deposed.  See Adams, *Shakespearean Playhouses*, pp. 356–62.

king's company usually brought out two or three new plays at the Globe every summer. (*Var.* iii. 153.)

As the Globe was partly exposed to the weather, and they acted there usually by day-light, it appeared to me probable (when this essay was originally published) that this was the summer theatre; and I have lately found my conjecture confirmed by Sir Henry Herbert's Manuscript. The king's company usually began to play at the Globe in the month of May. (*Var.* iii. 70–71.)

I have learned from Sir Henry Herbert's office-book, that between the years 1625 and 1641, [authors'] benefits were on the second day of representation. (*Var.* iii. 158.)

I have said in a former page, that I believed Sir George Buc died soon after the year 1622, and I have since found my conjecture confirmed. He died, as I learn from one of Sir Henry Herbert's papers, on the 20th of September,[1] 1623. (*Var.* iii. 181.)

"Meetinge with him [Beeston, the manager of the Cockpit Playhouse] at the ould exchange, he gave my wife a payre of gloves, that cost him at least twenty shillings." (*Var.* iii. 233.)

Hemings, however, it appears from Sir Henry Herbert's MS. took some concern in the management of the theatre, and used to present Sir Henry, as Master of the Revels, with his New-Year's gift for three or four years afterwards.[2] (Malone, *An Inquiry into the Authenticity of Certain Miscellaneous Papers*, 1796, p. 251.)

He was paid also particular gratuities for special services,[3] which he received for the last time, in June 1642; as the civil war was already begun. And, he possest what seems to have been a necessary appendage of his office, an appropriate box in the established theatres.[4] (*Apology*, 520 521.)

For licenses on all those accounts, the Master of the Revels

[1] The date given in the Dictionary of National Biography, and commonly by scholars, is September 22. This, apparently, is based on Chalmers, *S. A.*, p. 203. That the correct date is September 20 is shown by the *Declaration*, *May 6, 1662, Herbert and Thelwall versus Betterton*, see p. 109.
[2] I. e. after 1623, when, Malone assumes, Hemings retired from acting. Qy. for "New Year's gift" read "Christmas fee."
[3] See, for examples, pp. 64, 121.
[4] He claimed this after the Restoration; see pp. 122, 128.

required a fee; and a Christmas box of forty shillings, from each of the established theatres.[1]   (*S. A.* 209–210.)

Sir Henry Herbert exercised those extensive trusts, during a long life, through difficult times, with great discrimination of judgment, and firmness of decision. He, no doubt, received some useful assistance from George Wilson, who was sworn his Majesty's Servant, and a Groom of his Majesty's Revels, in ordinary, on the 4th of February, 1624–5.[2]  Whether this office of Groom of the Revels were distinct from the Yeoman of the Revels, I am unable to explain: Certain it is, that William Hunt, and after him, Joseph Taylor,[3] were Yeomen of the Revels, while George Wilson was the Groom.   With all those helps, Sir Henry Herbert's duty sometimes slept; owing to the multifarious nature of his office.   (*S. A.* 210–211.)

"The same day [Feb. 22, 1635][4] at Whitehall I acquainted king Charles, my master, with the danger of Mr. Hunts sickness, and moved his Majesty, in case he dyed, that he would be pleasd to give mee leave to commend a fitt man to succeed him in his place of Yeoman of the Revells.[5]

"The kinge tould me, that till then he knew not that Will Hunt held a place in the Revells.   To my request he was pleasd to give mee this answer.   Well, says the king, I will not dispose of it, or it shall not be disposed of, till I heare you.   *Ipsissimis verbis.*   Which I enter here as full of grace, and for my better remembrance, sinse *my master's custom affords not so many words, nor so significant."* [6]   (*Var.* iii. 238.)

[1] In 1663 he claimed "for Christmas fee, £3"; see p. 121.
[2] Chalmers in a footnote cites as his authority for this "Sir Henry Herbert's Official Register."
[3] The distinguished actor, a member of the King's Company, and one of the original performers of Hamlet; see Downes, *Roscius Anglicanus.*
[4] Possibly the correct date is February 25; see page 56, note 1.
[5] For a history of the office of yeoman see E. K. Chambers, *Notes on the History of the Revels Office under the Tudors.*
[6] In the papers of the Lord Chamberlain we find: "A warrant to swear M⟨r⟩ Joseph Taylor yeoman of the Revells to his Majesty in ordinary, in ye place of William Hunt, deceased. Sept. 29⟨th⟩ 1639." See Mrs. Stopes' extracts from the papers of the Lord Chamberlain, Shakespeare *Jahrbuch,* xlvi. 102; *Var.* iii. 218; Chalmers, *Apology,* p. 503. The patent, according to Cunningham, *Revels,* p. 1, is dated November 11, 1639. In Halliwell-Phillipps, *Collection,* p. 61, is a patent, dated June 1, 19 Charles II, appointing Henry Harris in the place of Taylor, the appointment dating from 1660.

# MISCELLANEOUS DOCUMENTS,
1622–1642

# MISCELLANEOUS DOCUMENTS,
## 1622–1642

The following documents, gathered from miscellaneous sources, further illustrate Herbert's connection with the Revels during the period 1622–1642. The two lists of Court plays acted by the King's Company are included because they confirm, correct, and supplement the lists given in the office-book.

## I. PAYMENT TO HERBERT FOR LODGING[1]

After my hearty comendacone: whereas, upon his Ma^{tie} Graunte of the house of S^t. Johns[2] unto the Lord Obigny,[3] there was order given for Allowance of fifty pounds by the yeare to bee made unto S^r George Bucke, Kn^t. dec^d., Master of His Ma^{ts} Revells, to provide himselfe of a convenient howse and office, to bee paid in his Accompts to bee yearely passed before you, as by warrants to you in that behalfe doth appeare. And for asmuch as S^r John Ashley, Kn^t., succeeding in the place of S^r George Bucke, doth as yet[4] provide himselfe of a howse and office at a yearely rent untill some other place shalbee assigned unto him for that purpose, and thereupon hath beene an humble suitor unto mee for such allowance as hath been formerly allowed to his predecessors, these are therefore to will and require you to allow unto him the sume of fifty pounds by the yeare, in his Accompts to bee passed before you, for two whole yeares ending at the feast of All Saints last past. And the same to continue yearely hereafter untill hee shalbee otherwise provided for by his Ma^{tie}. Whitehall, this last of June, 1624.

Yo^r loveing freind,

*Rich: Weston.*

To my very loving friends the Aud^{rs}
    of his Ma^{ts} Imprests.

[1] Printed by Cunningham, *Revels*, p. xxii, from *Enrolments*, vol. vi, p. 131. The order was reaffirmed after the Restoration, March 8, 1660, see Cunningham, *op. cit.*, p. xxvi.
[2] Which Elizabeth had set aside for the use of the Office of the Revels
[3] See p. 112.
[4] Ashley was, of course, technically still the Master of the Revels, although he had sold the position to Herbert.

## II.   PAYMENT TO HERBERT FOR LODGING [1]

*Warrant for the Payment of Fiftie-two Pounds to Sir Henry
Herbert, kt., Mr. of the Revells, for his lodgeinge out of Court
by the space of 52 Weekes, ended at our Ladie-daie last, 1627.*

WHEREAS you are authorized by virtue of his Majestie's
Letters Patents, beareinge date the 16th daie of June, 1625, made
and granted in confirmacion of diverse warrants and privie
seales unto you formelie directed in the tyme of our late deceased
sovereigne King James, (amongest other thinges) to make payment for the lodgings of such of his Majestie's servants as are
allowed them, and yet are not lodged within anie of his Highnes
houses: Theis are to pray and require you, out of his Majestie's
treasure in your charge, to paie, or cause to be paid, unto Sir
Henry Herbert, knighte, Master of his Majestie's Revells, the
some of fiftie and twoe pounds, being after the rate of xxs. a
weeke, for his lodgeing out of courte by the space of fiftie and
twoe weekes, viz. from the Feast of Annunciacion of our blessed
Virgin Marie, 1626, to the Feast of Annunciacion of our said
blessed Virgin Mary, next after followinge, 1627, as by his bill,
certified by Wm. Glover, esq., one of his Majestie's gentlemen
ushers and dailie wayters, hereto annexed, may appeare.   And
theis, togeither with his acquittance for the receipts thereof,
shall be your warrant.

Theobalds, this 17 of Julie, 1627.

MONGOMORIE.

To Sir William Uvedale, knight, Treasurer of
his Majestie's Chamber.

*Mensibus Martii, Aprilis, Marii, Junii, Julii, Augusti, Sep-
tembris, Octobr., Novembr., Decembr., Januar., Febr., et Martii,
annis 1626, et 1627, Annoque Regni Regis Caroli 2d, et 30.*

Sir Henry Herbert, knight, Mr. of his Majestie's Revells,
asketh allowance for his lodging, not being lodged in anie of his
Majestie's houses, by the space of fiftie-two weekes, viz. from
the Feast of the Annunciacion of our blessed Virgin Mary, 1626,
unto the Feast of the Annunciacion of the said blessed Virgin
next following, 1627, dureing which tyme he hath given his
attendance at Courte, and been at charges for his lodging dureing
the said tyme, in attending his said service, after the rate of

[1] Rebecca Warner, *Epistolary Curiosities*, Appendix, No. 1, p. 180.

xx *s.* per weeke, which he prayes maie bee paid unto him by the
Treasurer of his Majestie's Chamber. £52.

WILLIAM GLOVER.

### III. PAYMENT TO HERBERT FOR UNUSUAL ATTENDANCE[1]

After my very hartie commendacons. Whereas the Master
and Officers of the Revells were commaunded by his Ma[ty]
to beginne theire Attendaunce yearely at the feast of S[t]. Michaell
the Archaungell, which is above a moneth before their usuall
tyme of wayting, and demaund allowaunce for three late yeares
beginning the last of September 1630 and ending the last of
October 1632 a moneth sooner than their ordinary tyme of
attendaunce. Theis are therefore to pray and require you that
for every yeare within the said tyme you give allowaunce to the
Master of eight shillings per diem, which cometh to twelve
pounds. To the Clark Comptroller, Clerk, and Yeoman, three
pounds sixe shillings and eight pence a yeere, which comes to
tenne poundes, and to the Groome one pound thirteene shillings
fower pence yearely, and to contynue the same from tyme to
tyme yearely untill you have warraunt to the contrary. And for
so doing this shalbe your warraunte. Whitehall, the xiith of
Feb[y], 1636.

*Pembroke Mountgomerie.*

To my very loving friends the Auditors
 of his Mat[s]. Imprest, or any of them
 whome it may concerne.

[1] Printed by Cunningham, *Revels*, p. xxiii, from *Enrolments*, vol. iii, p. 750.
Chalmers, in his *Apology*, p. 506, prints this "from a MS. book in the Lord
Chamberlain's office," in a slightly different form. Cunningham and Chalmers
print also a similar order covering the period from October 1632 to October
1635. The order was again issued in 1660 covering the period from October
1660 to October 1666; see Cunningham, *op. cit.*, p. xxvi.

## IV.  DEMANDS OF HERBERT FOR WAGES, ETC.[1]

*The Demandes of Sir Henry Herbert, knight, for his wages and board wages, &c. as Master of the Revells to the late King.*

| | | | |
|---|---|---|---|
| Due to him the last of October, 1638, as appeares by the Auditor's Bookes of Accountes, and by a Privy Seale dated the sixthe of February, in the 16 yeare of the then Kinge Charles, the some of | 1065 | 12 | 10 |
| Due to him for dyet and boardinges, as appeares by the Auditor's Bookes of Accountes for 1639 | 230 | 0 | 0 |
| Due to him for the lyke for 1640, 1641, and 1642, being three yeares, the some of | 690 | 0 | 0 |
| Due to him for four years Fees, at £10 per annum, to 1643 | 40 | 0 | 0 |

Some is   £2025  12  10

## V.  HERBERT'S PROTECTIONS FROM ARREST[2]

Theise are to Certefie you That Edward Knight, William Pattrick, William Chambers, Ambrose Byland, Henry Wilson, Jeffery Collins, William Sanders, Nicholas Underhill, Henry Clay, George Vernon, Roberte Pallant, Thomas Tuckfeild, Roberte Clarke, John Rhodes, William Mago, Anthony Knight, and Edward Ashborne, William Carver, Allexander Buklank, William Toyer, William Gascoyne are all imployed by the Kinges Maiesties servantes in theire quallity of Playinge as Musitions and other necessary attendantes, And are att all tymes and howers to bee readie with theire best endeavours to doe his Maiesties service (dureinge the tyme of the Revells) In Which tyme they nor any of them are to bee arested, or deteyned vnder arest, imprisoned, Press'd for Souldiers, or any other molestation Whereby they may bee hindered from doeing his Maiesties service, Without leaue firste had and obteyned of the

---

[1] Rebecca Warner, *Epistolary Curiosities*, Appendix, No. 2, p. 182.

[2] Halliwell-Phillipps, *Collection*, p. 16.  Malone refers to the document, *Var.* iii. 112.  The British Museum Catalogue (Add. MSS. 19,256) describes it as "signed, and with seal," so that apparently it is the original document and not merely a copy.  By the Commission of 1581 Tilney had been granted the power to protect from arrest all persons connected with the revels at Court (see Feuillerat, *Documents*, p. 52), and this commission had been likewise issued to Astley.

Lord Chamberlyne of his Maiesties most honourable houshold, or of the Maister of his Maiesties Revells. And if any shall presume to interrupt or deteyne them or any of them after notice hereof given by this my Certificate, hee is to aunswere itt att his vtmost perill. Given att his Maiesties Office of the Revells vnder my hand and Seale the xxviith day of December, 1624.

H. HERBERT.

To all Mayors, Sheriffes, Justices of the Peace, Bayleiffes, Constables, knight Marshalls men, and all other his Maiesties Officers to whom it may or shall apperteyne.

A certificate graunted to Edward Shackerly not to bee arested or imprisoned dureing the tyme of the Revells, the 29th of Nouember 1624.

A certificate graunted to Richard Sharpe the 29° of December 1624 not to bee arested or imprisoned durcing the tyme of the Revells.

A Note of the Protections that have byn granted by mee.

## VI. COURT PLAYS, ACTED BY THE KING'S COMPANY, 1636–1637[1]

Playes acted before the Kinge and Queene
this present yeare of the lord. 1636.

1 Easter munday at the Cockpitt the firste parte of Arviragus
2 Easter tuesday at the Cockpitt the second parte of Arviragus
3 The 4$^{th}$ of Aprill at the Cockpitt the Silent woman.
4 The 5$^{th}$ of May at the Blackfryers for the Queene } Alfonso
   and the prince Elector

5 The 17$^{th}$ of November at Hampton Courte . the Coxcombe.
6 The 19$^{th}$ of November at Hampton Court . beggers bush.
7 The 29$^{th}$ of November at Hampton Court . the maides tragedie

[1] From the facsimile of the Audit Office document printed by Ernest Law in *More about Shakespeare "Forgeries."* See also Cunningham, *Revels*, p. xxiv This, and the following document, were bills presented by the King's Company for plays acted before the Court.

8 The 6ᵗʰ of December at Hampton Court . the loyall subiect.
9 The 8ᵗʰ of December at Hampton Court . the moore of Venice.
10 The 16ᵗʰ of December at Hampton Court . Loues pilgrimage
11 Sᵗ Stephens day at Hampton Court . the first pte of Arviragus.
12 Sᵗ Johns Day at Hampton Court . the second parte of Arviragus.
13 The first day of January at Hampton Court . loue and honor
14 The 5ᵗʰ of January at Hampton Court . the Elder brother.
15 The 10ᵗʰ of January at Hampton Court . the Kinge and noe Kinge.
16 The 12ᵗʰ of January the new play from Oxford . the Royall slave.
17 The 17ᵗʰ of January at Hampton Court———Rollo.
18 The 24ᵗʰ of January at Hampton Court———hamlett.

----

19 The 31ᵗʰ of January at Sᵗ James . the tragedie of Cesar.
20 The 9ᵗʰ of ffebruary at Sᵗ James . the wife for a moneth.
21 The 16ᵗʰ of ffebruary at Sᵗ James . the Governour.
22 The 21ᵗʰ of ffebruary at Sᵗ James . Philaster.

22 : playes.

## VII. COURT PLAYS, ACTED BY THE KING'S COMPANY, 1638–1639[1]

[Plays acted] before the king & queene this
[present] yeare of our lord 1638

At the Cocpit the 26ᵗʰ of march . . . . . . . . . . . . . . . .The lost ladie
At the Cocpit the 27ᵗʰ of march . . . . . . . . . . . . . . . . . .Damboyes
At the Cocpit the 3ᵈ of Aprill . . . . . . . . . . . . . . . . . . . . . .Aglaura
At the blackfryers the 23 of Aprill for the queene
                                    the vnfortunate lou[ers]
At the Cocpit the 29ᵗʰ of may the princes berthnight . .ould Castel
At the Cocpit the last of may agayne the . . . .vnfortunate louers
At Sumerset-house the 10ᵗʰ of July & our day
— lost at our house mʳ Carlels play the first part of the pasionate louers

[1] From the facsimile in *The Journal of the British Archæological Association*, 1860; also in *Archæologic and Historic Fragments*, by G. R. Wright, London, 1887.

— At Hamton Court the 30th of
    September . . . . . . . . . . . . . . . . . . . The vnfortunate louers

— At Richmount the 6th of ⎫
    november for the ladie  ⎪
    maries berthnight &   ⎬ . . The mery divell of Edmonto[n]
    the day lost at our    ⎪
    house                ⎭

At the Cocpit the 8th of november . . .              The fox

At the Cocpit the 13th of november . . . . . . . .     Ceaser

At the Cocpit the 15th of november . . . The mery wifes of winser

At the Cocpit the 20th of november . . .     .The fayre favorett

At the Cocpit the 22th of november . . .         Chances

At the Cocpit the 27th of november . The Costome of the C[ountry]

At the Cocpit the 29th of november . . . . . . . .The northern las

At the Cocpit the 6th of desember . . . . . . . . .The spanish Curatt

At the Cocpit the 11th of desember agayne . . . The fayre favorett

At the Cocpit the 18th of desember in Carlels
    play agayne the first part of . . . . . . . . . .The pasionate louers

At the Cocpit the 20th of desember the 2d
    part of . . . . . . . . . . . . . . . . . . . . . .The pasionate louers

At the Cocpit the 27 of desember the 2d
    part agayne of            the pasionate louers

— At Richmount the 28 of desember the ⎫
    ladie Elsabeths berthnight & our day ⎬. . The northern las
    lost at our house             ⎭

— At Richmount on newyeares day ⎫ . . . . beggers bush
    and our day lost at our house ⎭

— At Richmount the 7th of Janeuarye ⎫ .The spanish Cura[tt][1]
    and our day lost at our house ⎭

[1] The checks at the left were made by the Lord Chamberlain to ascertain how many times the actors lost their day at their house, and hence were entitled to a payment of £20 instead of the customary £10. The performance at Blackfriars was at night, so that the actors did not lose their daily income from the public, and hence received from the Lord Chamberlain only £10. For a general discussion see Adams, *Shakespearean Playhouses*, pp. 232-33.

# MISCELLANEOUS DOCUMENTS,
## 1660–1670

# MISCELLANEOUS DOCUMENTS,
## 1660–1670

## I. LICENSE OF SALISBURY COURT PLAYHOUSE[1]

Whereas the allowance of Playes, the ordering of Players and Playmakers, and the Permission for Errecting of Playhouses, Hath, time out of minde whereof the memory of man is not to the Contrary, belonged to the Master of his Majesties Office of the Revells.

And whereas Mister William Beeston hath desired Authority and Lycence from mee to Continue the house called Salsbury Court Play house In a Playhouse, which was formerly built and Errected into a Playhouse by the Permission and Lycence of the Master of the Revells.

These are therefore by vertue of a Grante vnder the Greate Seale of England, and of the Constant Practice thereof, to Continue and Constitute the said house called Salisbury Court Play house into a Play house, and to Authorize and Lycence the said Mister Beeston to Sett, Lett, or vse it for a Play house, wherein Comedies, tragedies, trage Comedies, Pastoralls, and Interludes, may bee Acted, Prouided that noe persons be admitted to Act in the said Play house but such as shall be allowed by the Master of his Majesties Office of the Revells. Given under my hand and Seale of the office of the Revells, this

For Mister William Beeston.

## II. COPY OF A WARRANT GRANTED TO FENCERS[2]

With the favour and priviledge of his Highnes the Duke of Yorke, it is agreed upon, by, and betweene Francis Burges and William Tubb, to play a tryall of skill at eight severall weapons, which are hereunder expressed, on the thirteenth day of August next, being Monday, at the Red Bull Playhouse.—30th July, 1660.

---

[1] Halliwell-Phillipps, *Collection*, p. 85; Ma'one, *Var.* iii 243. Malone says: "This paper appears to be only a copy, and is not dated nor signed ending as above. I believe, it was written in June, 1660."

[2] Rebecca Warner, *Epistolary Curiosities*, Appendix, No. 3, p. 183

| *The Weapons of Francis Burges* | *The Weapons of Wm. Tubb* |
|---|---|
| Backe Sword | Single Rapier |
| Sword and Gantlet | Rapier and Dagger |
| Sword and Dagger | Halfe Pike |
| Sword and Buckler. | Quarter Staffe. |

Whereas his Highness, the Duke of Yorke, hath been pleased to commende unto me Francis Burges and Wm. Tubb, for a warrant to playe a prize,

These are to authorize the said Francis Burges and William Tubb to playe a prize at the weapons above named, at the House called the Red Bull, and for so doinge this shall be their warant.

Dated the 30th July, 1660.

· H. HERBERT.

## III.   RED BULL PLAYS[1]

Names of the plays acted by the Red Bull actors.

| | |
|---|---|
| The Humorous Lieutenant. | Elder Brother. |
| Beggars Bushe. | The Silent Woman. |
| Tamer Tamed. | The Weddinge. |
| The Traytor. | Henry the Fourthe. |
| Loves Cruelty. | Merry Wives of Windsor. |
| Wit without Money. | Kinge and no Kinge. |
| Maydes Tragedy. | Othello. |
| Philaster. | Dumboys. |
| Rollo Duke of Normandy. | The Unfortunate Lovers. |
| Claricilla. | The Widow. |

[1] *Var.* iii. 272. This is not in Halliwell-Phillipps's *Collection*. Malone introduces it with the following comment: "The actors who had performed at the Red Bull, acted under the direction of Mr. Killegrew during the years 1660, 1661, 1662, and part of the year 1663, in Gibbon's tennis-court in Vere Street, near Clare-market; during which time a new theatre was built for them in Drury Lane, to which they removed in April, 1663. The following list of their stock-plays, in which it is observable there are but three of Shakspeare, was found among the papers of Sir Henry Herbert, and was probably furnished by them soon after the Restoration." I have given the order in which the plays are printed in the 1790 edition of Malone. The list should be studied in connection with the lists on page 116, and in John Downes's *Roscius Anglicanus*.

## IV. PETITION OF JOHN ROGERS, AND HERBERT'S ORDER RELATING THERETO[1]

To the Kings most Excellent Maiesty.
The humble Peticion of John Rogers,
Most humbly Sheweth,
That your Peticioner at the beginning of the late Calametys lost thereby his whole Estate, and during the Wars Susteyned muche detriment and Imprisonment, and Lost his Limbs and the vse thereof; who served his Excellency the now Lord Generall, both in England and Scotland, and performed good and faithtull Service; In Consideracion whereof, and by being soe much Decreapitt as not to act any more in the wars, his Excellency was fauourably pleased, for your Peticioners future Subsistance without being further burthensome to this Kingdom, or to your Majesty for a Pencion, To grant him a Tolleration to erect a playhouse or to haue a share out of them already Tollerated, your Peticioner thereby vndertaking to Supres all Riotts, Tumults, or Molestacions that may thereby arise. And for that the said Graunt Remains Imperfect vnles Corroborated by your Majesty,
He therefore humbly Implors your most Sacred Maiesty, in Tender Compassion, out of your Kingly Clemency to Confirm vnto him a share out of the Profitts of the said Playhouses, or such allowance by them to be giuen as formerly they vsed to alow to persons for to keepe the Peace of the same, that he may with his wife and famely be thereby Preserued and Releiued in his maimed, aged yearrs; And he shall Dayly pray, &c.
At the Court at Whitehall the 7th of August 1660.[2]

His Majesty is Graciously pleased to Refer this Peticion to Sir Henry Herbert, Master of his Majestis Revells, to take such order therein, as shalbe agreable to Equety, without further trubling his Majesty.

J. HOLLIS.

A true Copye August 20, 1660, From the office of the Reuells

In obedience to his Majesties Reference I Have taken the matter of the Petitioners Request Into Consideration, And conceive it reasonable That the Petitioner should haue the same Allowance weekly from your Playhouse which you doe allowe

---

[1] Halliwell-Phillipps, *Collection*, p. 17; Malone, *Var.* iii. 244
[2] For a later reference to Rogers see p. 127.

Other Persons for the same worke. To the Actors at the Red-bull, and to euery of them.[1]

In obedience to his Majesties Comands I haue taken the Matter of the peticioners request into Consideration, and doe therevpon Conceiue it very reasonable that the peticioner should haue the same allowance weekely from you and euery of you, for himselfe and his men, for Guarding your playhouses from all Molestations and Iniuries, which you formerly did or doe allow or pay to other persons for the saime or such like seruices; and that it be duly and truely paid him without deniall. And the rather for that the Kings most excellent Majestie vpon the Lord Generall Monks recomendation, And the Consideracion of the peticioners Losses and Sufferings, hath thought fitt to Commisserate the Peticionour John Rogers his said Condicion, and to refferr vnto me the releif of the said peticioner.

Given at his Majesties office of the Revells, vnder my hand and the Seale of the said office, the twentith day of August, in the tweluth yeare of his Majesties Raigne.

> To the Actors of the Playhouses called the
> Red bull, Cockpitt, and Theatre in Salesbury
> Court, and to euery of them, in & about the
> Citties of London & Westminster.

## V. SUBMISSION OF PLAYERS TO HERBERT'S AUTHORITY[2]

Wee, whose names are here vnderwritten, doe hereby promise and Couenant to pay or cause to be paid to Sir Henry Herbert, Knight, Master of his Majesties Office of the Reuells, or to his Deputy, or Agent, the summe of ten pounds on saturday next after the Date herof. And what Plaies soeuer wee shall Act for the future, to pay or cause to be paid to the said Sir Henry Herbert, his Deputy, or Agent, for euery new Play 40s., and for euery reuiued Play 20s., as fees antiently belonging to the Master of the Reuells. And wee doe hereby further [promise, swe]are, and Couenant to pay, or cause to bee [paid, the said s]umme to the said Master of the Reuells, his [Deputy, or Ag]ent,

---

[1] This paragraph was omitted by Malone. Probably Herbert substituted for it the paragraph that follows, directed to the actors not only at the Red Bull but also at the Cockpit and Salisbury Court.

[2] Halliwell-Phillipps, *Collection*, p. 36.

on euery Saturday successively [beginning from this date herof
In Witnesse wherof wee have herevnto sett our handes and
seales this 14 August, 1660. These Couenantes are to be made
good during the time of acting vnder the said Master of the
Reuells.

   a true Copy

NICH. BURTT

## VI. HERBERT'S PROTEST AGAINST THE PROPOSED GRANT TO KILLIGREW AND DAVENANT[1]

   To the Kings most Excellent Maiestie. The humble
peticion of Sir Henry Herbert, Knight, Master of your
Maiesties Office of the Revells.

   Sheweth,

   That whereas your petitioner by vertue of seuerall graunts
vnder the great seale of England hath executed the said Office
as Master of the Revells, for about 40 yeares, in the times of
King James, and of King Charles, both of blessed memory,
with excepcion only to the time of the late horrid rebellion.

   And whereas the ordering of plaies, players, and play makers,
and the permission for erecting of playhouses are Peculiar
branches of the said Office, and in the constant Practice thereof
by your petitioner's Predecessors in the said Office and himselfe,
with excepcion only as before excepted, and authorised by
graunt vnder the said great seale of England; and that no person
or persons haue erected any Playhouses, or raised any Company
of Players, without Licence from your petitioner's said Predecessors or from your petitioner, But Sir William Davenant,
Knight, who obtained Leaue of Oliver and Richard Cromwell to
vent his Operas, in a time when your petitioner owned not their
Authority.

   And whereas your Maiesty hath lately signified your pleasure
by warrant to Sir Jefferry Palmer, Knight and Barronet, your
Majesties Attorney Generall, for the drawing of a graunt for
your Majesties signature to pass the greate seale, thereby to
enable and impower Mister Thomas Killegrew and the said Sir
William Davenant to erect two new Playhouses in London,
Westminster, or the Subburbs thereof, and to make Choice of

[1] Halliwell-Phillipps, *Collection*, p. 21; Malone, *Var.* iii. 246. Halliwell-
Phillipps prints a second copy of the petition, p. 23, but since this offers no
variations, I have not reproduced it.

Two Companies of Players, to bee vnder theire sole regulacion, and that noe other players shalbee authorized to play in London, Westminster, or the Subburbs thereof but such as the said Mister Killegrew and Sir William Davenant shall allow of.

And whereas your petitioner hath been represented to your Maiesty as a person consenting to the said powers expressed in the said Warrant, your petitioner vtterly denies the least Consent or foreknowledge thereof, but look vpon it as an vniust surprize, and distructiue to the powers graunted vnder the said great seale to your petitioner, and to the Constant practice of the said Office, and exercised in the said Office ever since Players were first admitted by authority to act plaies, and cannot legally bee done as your petitioner is advised; and it may bee of very ill consequence, as your petitioner is advised, by a new graunt to take away and cut off a braunch of the antient powers graunted to the said Office vnder the great seale.

Your petitioner therefore humbly praies that your Maiesty would bee iustly as graciously pleased to revoke the said Warrant from your Maiesties said Attorney Generall, Or to referr the premises to the consideracion of your Maiesties said Attorney Generall to Certify your Maiesty of the truth of them, and his Judgment on the whole matters in question betwixt the said Mister Killigrew, Sir William Davenant, and your petitioner, in relacion to the Legallity and Consequence of theire demaunds and your petitioners rights.

And your petitioner shall ever pray, etc.

At the Court at Whitehall, 4 Augusti, 1660.

His Maiestie is pleased to referre this Peticion to Sir Jeffery Palmer, Knight and Baronet, his Maiesties Atturney generall; who hauing called before him all Persons concerned, and examined the Peticioners right, is to certify what hee finds to bee the true state of the matters in difference, together with his opinion thereupon. And then his Maiestie will declare his further pleasure.

EDWARD NICHOLAS.

May it please your most excellent Maiesty:

Although I haue heard the Parties concerned in this Peticion seuerally and apart, yet in respect Mister Killigrew and Sir William Dauenant, haueing notice of a time appointed to heare all parties together did not come, I haue forborne to proceede further; haueing alsoe receaued an intimacion, by Letter from

Sir William Dauenant, that I was freed from further hearing this matter.

14° Sept. 1660.

G. PALMER.[1]

## VII. THE KING'S GRANT TO KILLIGREW AND DAVENANT[2]

Charles the Second, by the Grace of God, of England, Scotland, ffrance and Ireland, King, defender of the ffayth, &c., To all to whome these presents shall Come, Greeting. Whereas wee are giuen to vnderstand that Certaine persons In and about Our Citty of London, or the Suburbs thereof, Doe frequently assemble for the performing and Acting of Playes and Enterludes for Rewards, To which diuers of Our Subiects doe for theire Entertainment Resort; which said playes, As wee are Informed, doe Containe much Matter of Prophanation, and Scurrility, soe that such Kind of Entertainments, which, if well Mannaged, might serue as Morrall Instructions In Humanne life, As the same are now vsed, doe for the most part tende to the Debauch-inge of the Manners of Such as are present at them, and are very Scandalous and offensive to all pious and well disposed persons. Wee, takeing the premisses into our Princely Consideration, yett not holding it necessary totally to Suppresse the vse of theatres, because wee are assured, that, if the Evill & Scandall In the Playes that now are or haue bin acted were taken away, the same might serue as Innocent and Harmlesse diuertisements for many of our Subiects; And Haueing Experience of the Art and skill of our Trusty and welbeloved Thomas Killegrew, Esquire, one of the Groomes of our Bedchamber, and of Sir William Dauenant, Knight, for the purposses hereafter men-cioned, Doe hereby giue & Grante vnto the said Thomas Kille-grew and Sir William Dauenant full power & authority to Erect two Companies of Players, Consistinge respectiuely of such persons As they shall chuse and appoint, And to purchase, builde and Erect, or hire at their Charge, As they shall thinke fitt, two Houses or theatres, withall Convenient Roomes and other Necessaries therevnto appertaining for the Representation of Tragydies, Comedyes, Playes, Operas, & all other Entertain-

---

[1] Malone has "J. Palmer."
[2] Halliwell-Phillipps, *Collection*, p. 19; Malone, *Var.* iii. 249

ments of that nature, In Convenient places: And likewise to
Setle and Esstablish such payments to be paid by those that
shall resort to see the said Representations performed, As either
haue bin accustomely Giuen and taken in the like Kind, or as
shall be reasonable In regard of the Great Expences of Scenes,
musick and such new Decorations as Have not been formerly
used; with further power to make such allowances out of that
which they shall so receiue, to the Actors, and other persons
Employed In the said Representations in both houses Respectively, As they shall thinke fitt: the said Companies to be vnder
the Gouernement and Authority of them the said Thomas
Killegrew and Sir William Dauenant. And In regard of the
Extraordinary Licentiousness that hath benn Lately used In
things of this nature, Our Pleasure Is that there shall be noe more
Places of Representations, nor Companies of Actors of Playes,
or Operas by Recitative musick, or Representations by danceing
and Scenes, or any other Entertainments on the Stage, In our
Cities of London and Westminster, or in the Liberties of them,
then the two to be now Erected by vertue of this Authority.
Neuertheless wee doe Hereby by our Authority Royal strictly
enioine the said Thomas Killegrew and Sir William Dauenant
that they doe not at any time Herafter cause to be acted or
represented any Play, Enterlude, or opera, Containing any
Matter of Prophanation, Scurrility or Obscenity: And wee doe
further Hereby authorize and Command them the said Thomas
Killegrew and Sir William Dauenant, to peruse all playes that
haue been formerly written, and to expunge all Prophanesse
and Scurrility from the same, before they be represented or
Acted. And this Our Grante and Authority made to the said
Thomas Killegrew and Sir William Davenant, shall be effectuall
and Remaine in full force and vertue, Notwithstanding any
former order or direction by vs Given, for the Suppressing of
Playhouses and playes, or any other Entertainments of the
Stage. Given[1] August 21st, 1660.

Copy of the grante the 21 August. 60. made to Mister Thomas
Killegrew and Sir William Dauenant by the Kings Maiesty,
under the Priuy Signett.[2]

[1] Malone reads "Give, &c."
[2] Malone omits this last paragraph.

## VIII. HERBERT'S "ANSWER" TO THE GRANT [1]

Abstracte of the Powers granted to Mister Thomas Killegrew and sir william Dauenant by warant directed to His Maiesties Aturney Generall.

To erecte two new Playhouses In London, Westminster, or the suburbes therof.

To raise two new Companies and to haue the sole Regulation of them.

That noe other Playhouses shall be Allowed of nor any other Players but such as shall be Authorized by them.

### Sir Henry Herberts Answer
### Master of His Maiesties office of the Reuells

That the Licensinge and Orderinge of Playes, Players, and Playmakers, and for Erecting of Playhouses Is an Antient Branche of His Maiesties office of the Reuells, and Hath ben soly exercised by the present master of the Reuells and His Predecessors tyme out of minde, with exception only to the time of the Late Horrid Rebellion, when sir Henry Herbert owned not their uniust and Tyranicall Authority, thogh sir william Dauenant did, and obteyned then Leaue to uente his Operas.

That the Grante of the forenamed Powers Is Destructiue to the Powers granted under the Great Seale to sir Henry Herbert by the Late Kinge of Blessed Memory, And to the constant practise of the said office.

That It is Destructiue to a Hundred Persons at Least that depende upon the Quality and the Houses and Haue noe other Liuelyhood.

That it cannot Legally be done, As Councell doth Aduise, and being granted begets a Suite at Law upon the Validity of the Grantes.

[1] Halliwell-Phillipps, *Collection*, p. 33.

## IX.  LETTER FROM HUMPHREY MOSELY, CONCERNING PLAYS THAT BELONG TO HIM [1]

From Mr. Mosely concerning the playes, &c.<br>
August 30, 1660.[2]

Sir,

I have beene very much solicited by the gentlemen actors of the Red Bull for a note under my hand to certifie unto your worsh[p]. what agreement I had made with Mr. Rhodes, of the Cockpitt playhouse.  Truly, Sir, I am so farr from any agreement with him, that I never so much as treated with him, nor with any from him, neither did I ever consent directly or indirectly, that hee or any others should act any playes that doe belong to mee, without my knowledge and consent had and procured.  And the same also I doe certify concerning the Whitefryers playhouse and players.

Sir, this is all I have to trouble you withall att present, and therefore I shall take the boldnesse to remaine,

Your Worsh[s]. most humble Servant,<br>
HUMPHREY  MOSELY.

August 30. 60.[3]

## X.  FROM THE MAYOR AND RECORDER OF MAIDSTONE, TO SIR HENRY HERBERT [4]

*Maidstone, 8th Oct. 1660.*

Honorable Sir,—We received youres of the sixth instant by these bearers, and question not your commission as Master of his Majestie's Revells, or your licence granted to these persons, Jacob Brewer, &c.; nor them, so farre as they shall use the same according to lawe, to which your license doth prudently and carefully tye them.  One particular of which theyre lawfull exercise we conceive to be within the verge of his Majestie's courte, wherever it shall be, in any parte of Englande, where they may be under your eye and care, for the reforminge and

---

[1] Malone, *Var.* iii. 249.

[2] "This is the endorsement, written in Sir Henry Herbert's own hand."—Malone.

[3] "The date inserted by Sir Henry Herbert."—Malone.

[4] Rebecca Warner, *Epistolary Curiosities*, p. 59.

regulating any abuses of their license which might be committed by them. But we doe not finde that you doe, and presume you did not intend to grant them a licence to wander abroade all England over, at what distance soever from you. And we finde that the wanderinge abroad of such persons is expresslye cautioned by the statut of the 39th of the Queen,[1] in the case of players of interludes and minstrels (except it be by expresse license under the hande and seale of such Baron, or other noble person of greater degree, to whome they doe particularly belonge); and however we knowe no lawe or statut that requires the magistrates of any place to give them any particular leave or license of theyre owne by way of addition to any other. And, indeed, the mischiefe and publicke disorders by the practices of such kinde of persons in wanderinge abroade from countye to countye, is such that we cannot thinke it reasonable to give them any further countenance than the lawe provides; which we hope will not be displeasing to you, who, we presume, do take the observance of his Majestie's lawes to the best obedience to his Majestie's authoritye. In which assurance we take leave, and rest, Honourable Sir, youre most humble servants.

RICHARD BILLS, Maior.
LAMBARDE GODFREY, Recorder.

To the Hon. Sir Henry Herbert, knight, Master of his Majestie's Revells, these humbly present.

(*Endorsed*)—From the Maior of Maydstone, and the Recorder, concer. Jacob Brewer, dancer on the ropes.

## XI. FROM SIR H. HERBERT TO THE MAYOR OF MAIDSTONE[2]

*Oct. 9,—60, from the Office of the Revells.*

Sir,—Yours of the 8th comes to my hande the 9th of this monthe, and makes out an acknowledgment and submission to his Majestie's grante, as Master of his Majestie's Revells, and to the powers of lycencinge the persons in question, and to their exercise of the said powers, so farr as they shall use the same according unto lawe: but you restraine the exercise thereof to

---

[1] Queen Elizabeth. The statute has been reprinted in W. C. Hazlitt's *The English Drama and Stage*, p. 37; cf. also p. 21.
[2] Rebecca Warner, *Epistolary Curiosities*, p. 61; see British Museum Addit. MS. 37157, f. 64.

the verge of his Majestie's court, and then restraine the Master of the Revells to the said limits, as to his jurisdiction; which is, in some sort, a contradiction; and such an interpretation as was never given before by any learned gentlemen. The license is granted upon the conditions of good behaviour to the lawes and ordinances of superiors. But you are not taken to be in a capacity, by virtue of your charter, to suppresse them, they bearinge themselves as they ought to doe. And there is *non obstante* in the concession which provides against the penall lawes, which being under the greate seale of England, and corroborated by a constant practice, whereof the memorie of man is not to the contrarie, I conceive you will not be the sole infringer of his Majestie's grante, and the constant practice thereof in all his Majestie's dominions and liberties in England. And you may be assured by me that you are the first mayor, or other officer, that ever did dispute the authority, or the extent of it; for to confine it to the verge of the Court is such a sense as was never imposed upon it before, and contrary to the constant practice; for severall grantes have been made by me since the happy restoration of our gracious sovereign, to persons in the like quality; and seriously, therefore, admitted into all the counties and liberties of England without any dispute or molestation.

You are, therefore, desired to give them leave to exercise their qualities accordinge to the conditions of their license, the rather that they have suffered muche in lyinge still, and are in their waye to the sea syde for transportation; and I have given them order to stay noe longer than they have raysed their necessayre charges. But in case you doe delyghte in opposition and obstinacy to lawfull authority and yet would be obeyed in yours without dispute; then you may take this from me, that I shall forthwith sende a message from his Majestie's chamber to fetche you and Mr. Recorder Godfrey hither to answer your disobedience to his Majestie's authority derived unto me under the great seale of England, and in exercise of the said powers by me for almost forty yeares, with exception only to the late times. And if you have endangered your charter by this refracteriness, and doe put charges and displeasures on your corporation and persons, you will remember that you were faierly invited to the contrary, and admonished thereof by your very affectionate friend,

HENRY HERBERT.

Respects to Mr. Recorder Godfrey, of whom I have hearde well by my cosen Lambert, and for whom I have particular kindnes.

## XII. HERBERT ATTEMPTS TO ESTABLISH HIS AUTHORITY OVER THE COCKPIT PLAYHOUSE[1]

Whereas by vertue of a Grante vnder the Greate Scale of England, Playes, Players and Playmakers, and the Permission for Errecting of Playhouses, haue been allowed, Ordered and Permitted by the Masters of his Maiesties Office of the Revells, my Predecessors successively, time out of minde, whereof the memory of mann is not to the Contrary, And by mee for almost fforty yeares, with Exception only to the Late times:

These are therefore in his Maiesties name to require you to attende mee concerning your Playhouse called the Cockpitt Playhouse in Drury Lane, And to bring with you such Authority As you haue for Errecting of the said house Into a Playhouse, at your perill. Given at his Majesties Office of the Revells the 8th day of October 1660.

HENRY HERBERT.

To Mister John Roades at the Cockpitt Playhouse in Drury Lane.

Warrant sent to Rhodes and brought backe by him the 10th of October 1660 with this Answer: That the Kinge did authorize Him.[2]

## XIII. A SECOND LETTER TO THE COCKPIT PLAYERS[3]

Copy of the Warrant sent to the actors at the Cockpitt in Drury Lane by Tom Browne, the 13 Octob. 60.

Whereas severall complaints have been made against you to the Kings most excellent Majesty by Mr. Killegrew and Sir William D'Avenant, concerning the unusuall and unreasonable rates taken at your playhouse doores, of the respective persons of quality that desire to refresh or improve themselves by the sight of your morrall entertainments which were constituted for

---

[1] Halliwell-Phillipps, *Collection*, p. 26; Malone, *Var* iii 252.

[2] Malone places this last paragraph at the head of the document. He states that it is in the hand of Sir Henry Herbert.

[3] Malone, *Var.* iii. 252. This letter should be read in connection with the Grant to Davenant and Killigrew, p. 87.

profitt and delight.   And the said complaints made use of by
the said Mr. Killegrew and Sir William Davenant as part of
their suggestions for their pretended power, and for your late
restrainte.

And whereas complaints have been made thereof formerly to
mee, wherewith you were acquainted, as innovations and exactions not allowed by mee; and that the like complaints are
now made, that you do practice the said exactions in takeing of
excessive and unaccustomed rates uppon the restitution of you
to your liberty.

These are therefore in his Ma.<sup>ties</sup> name to require you and
every of you to take from the persons of qualitie and others
as daily frequent your playhouse, such usuall and accustomed
rates only as were formerly taken at the Blackfryers by the late
company of actors there, and noe more nor otherwise, for every
new or old play that shall be allowed you by the Master of the
Revells to be acted in the said playhouse or any other playhouse.
*And you are hereby further required to bringe or sende to me all
such old plaies as you doe intend to act at your said playhouse,
that they may be reformed of prophanes and ribaldry, at your perill.
Given at the office of the Revells.*[1]

HENRY HERBERT.

To Mr. Michael Mohun,
and the rest of the actors
of the Cockpitt playhouse
in Drury Lane.   The 13th
of October, 1660.

## XIV.  THE PETITION OF THE COCKPIT PLAYERS[2]

To the Kings most excellent Majestie.

The humble Petition of Michael Mohun, Robert Shatterell,
Charles Hart, Nich. Burt, Wm. Cartwright, Walter Clun, and
William Wintersell.

---

[1] "The words in Italick characters were added by Sir Henry Herbert's
own hand."—Malone.

[2] Malone, *Var.* iii. 254; Halliwell-Phillipps, *Collection*, p. 44.  Since the
manuscript seems to have been more legible when Malone copied it, and since
his transcript is obviously more correct, I have reproduced it; the variants
in Halliwell-Phillipps's transcript I have recorded in footnotes.

Humbly sheweth,

That your Majesties humble petitioners, having been supprest by a warrant from your Majestie, Sir Henry Herbert informed us it was Mr. Killegrew had caused it, and if wee would give him soe much a weeke, he would protect them against Mr. Killegrew and all powers. The complaint against us was, scandalous plays, raising the price, and acknowledging noe authority; all which ended in soe much per[1] weeke to him; for which wee had leave[2] to play, and promise of his protection: the which your Majesty knows he was not able to performe, since Mr. Killegrew, having your Majesties former grante, supprest us, until wee had by covenant obliged ourselves to act with woemen, a new theatre, and habitts according to our sceanes. And according to your Majesties approbation, from all the companies we made election of one company; and so farre Sir Henry Herbert hath bene from protecting us, that he hath been a continual disturbance unto us, who were [united][3] by your Majesties commande under Mr. Killegrew, as Master of your Majesties Comedians;[4] and we have annext unto our petition the date of the warrant by which wee were supprest, and for a protection against that warrant he forced from us[5] soe much a weeke. And if your majestie be graciously pleased to cast your eye upon the date of the warrant hereto annext, your majestie shall find the date to our contract[6] succeeded; wherein he hath broke the covenants, and not your petitioners,[7] haveing abused your majestie in giveing an ill character of your petitioners, only to force a sum from their poor endeavours: who never did nor shall refuse him all the reseits[8] and just profitts that belong to his place: hee having now obtained leave to arrest us, only to give trouble and vexation to your petitioners, hopeing by that meanes to force a summe of money illegally from us.

The premises considered, your petitioners humbly beseech your majestie to be gratiously pleased to signify your royal pleasure to the Lord Chamberlaine, that your petitioners

---

[1] *Collection*, "the."
[2] *Collection*, "his leave."
[3] *Collection*, "there establisht."
[4] *Collection*, "Revels."
[5] *Collection*, "first paid at" for "forced from us."
[6] *Collection*, "one that" for "our contract"; apparently the manuscript had decayed since Malone saw it.
[7] *Collection*, "Majestie," which is obviously wrong.
[8] *Collection*, "resarts."

may not bee molested in their calling.   And your petitioners in duty bound shall pray, &c.

NICH. BURT.                                ROBT. SHATTEREL.
WILLIAM WINTERSHALL.
CHARLES HART.

The 13 of [October 1660]

Confer[ence] Had with the [King conc]erninge Killigrew [and the P]layers.[1]

## XV.  ARTICLES OF AGREEMENT BETWEEN DAVE-NANT AND THE COMPANY OF PLAYERS AT THE COCKPIT [2]

Articles of Agreement tripartite, Indented, made, and agreed vppon this fifth Day of Nouember, in the xiith yeare of the reigne of our Souereigne Lord Kinge Charles the second, Annoque Domini 1660, Between Sir William Davenant, of London, Knight, of the first part, and Thomas Batterton, Thomas Sheppey, Robert Noakes, James Noakes, Thomas Lovell, John Moseley, Caue Vnderhill, Robert Turner, and Thomas Lilleston, of the second part; and Henry Harris, of the City of London, painter,[3] of the third part, as followeth.

Imprimis, the said Sir William Davenant doth for himself, his Executors, administrators and assignes, Couenant, promise, grant, and agree, to and with the said Thomas Batterton, Thomas Sheppey, Robert Noakes, James Noakes, Thomas Louell, John Mosely, Cave Vnderhill, Robert Turner, and Thomas Lilleston, that hee the said Sir William Davenant by vertue of the authority to him deriued for that purpose does[4] hereby constitute, ordeine, and erect them the said Thomas Batterton, Thomas Sheppey, Robert Noakes, James Noakes, Thomas Louell, John Moseley, Cave Vnderhill, Robert Turner, and Thomas Lilleston and their Associates, to bee a company,

---

[1] This postscript, omitted by Malone, I add from *A Collection*.  For the answer to this petition see Chalmers, *Apology*, p. 529.
[2] Printed in Halliwell-Phillipps, *Collection*, p. 27, and in Malone, *Var.* iii. 257.   This copy of the Articles of Agreement was made for Herbert's use in his lawsuits; see pp. 106, 112.
[3] Halliwell-Phillipps reads "panter," Malone "painter."
[4] Halliwell-Phillipps reads "doe," Malone "does."

publiquely to act all manner of Tragedies, Comedies, and playes whatsoeuer, in any Theatre or Playhouse erected in London or Westminster or the Subvrbs thereof, and to take the vsual rates for the same, to the vses hereafter exprest, vntill the said Sir William Davenant shall prouide a newe Theatre with Scenes.

Item, It is agreed by and betweene all the said parties to these presentes, that the said Company, (vntill the said theatre bee prouided by the said Sir William Davenant) be authorized by him to Act Tragedies, Comedies, and playes in the Playhouse called Salisbury Court Playhouse, or any other house, vpon the Condicions onely hereafter followeing, vizt.

That the generall receiptes of money of the said playhouse shall (after the houserent, hirelinges, and all other accustomary and necessary expenses in that kind bee defrayed) bee devided into fowerteene proporcions or shares, whereof Sir[1] William Davenant shall haue fowre full proporcions or shares to his owne vse, and the rest to the vse of the said Companie.

That dureinge the time of playeing in the said Playhouse, (vntill the aforesaid Theatre bee prouided by the said Sir William Davenant) the said Sir Wm. Davenant shall depute the said Thomas Batterton, James Noakes, and Thomas Sheppey, or any one of them perticularly, for him and on his behalf, to receiue his proporcion of those shares, and to survey the accomptes conduceing therevnto and to pay the said proporcion euery night to him the said Sir William Davenant or his assignes, which they doe hereby Couenant to pay accordingly.

That the said Thomas Batterton, Thomas Sheppey, and the rest of the said Company shall admitt such a Consort of Musiciens into the said Playhouse for their necessary vse, as the said Sir William shall nominate and provide, duringe their playinge in the said Playehouse, not exceedinge the rate of 30s. the day, to bee defrayed out of the generall expences of the house before the said fowerteene shares bee devided.

That the said Thomas Batterton, Thomas Sheppey, and the rest of the said Companie soe authorized to play in the Playhouse in Salisbury Court or elsewhere, as aforesaid, shall at one weeks warneinge giuen by the said Sir William Davenant, his heires or assignes, dissolue and conclude their Playeing at the house and place aforesaid, or at any other house where they shall play, and shall remove and Joyne with the said Henry Harris, and with other men and women prouided or to be prouided by the said Sir Wm. Davenant, to performe such Tragedies,

[1] Malone reads "the said Sir."

8

Comedies, Playes, and representacions in that Theatre to be publiquely[1] prouided by him the said Sir William as aforesaid.

Item, it is agreed by and betweene all the said parties to these presents in manner and forme followeinge (videlicet) That when the said Companie, together with the said Henry Harris, are ioyned with the men and women to be prouided by the said Sir William Davenant to Act and performe in the said Theatre to bee prouided by the said Sir William Davenant, That then[2] the generall receiptes of the said Theatre (the generall expence first beinge deducted) shalbee deuided into fifteene shares or proporcions, whereof two shares or proporcions shalbee paid to the said Sir William Davenant, his Executors, administrators, or assigns, towardes the house-rent, buildinge, scaffoldinge, and makeing of fframes for Scenes, And one other share or proporcion shall likewise bee paid to the said Sir William, his executors, administrators and assignes, for provision of Habittes, Properties, and scenes, for a Supplement of the said Theatre.

That the other twelve shares (after all expences of men hirelinges and other customary expences deducted) shalbee deuided into seauen and fiue shares or proportions, whereof the said Sir Wm. Davenant, his Executors, administrators, or assignes, shall have seauen shares or proporcions, to mainteine all the Women that are to performe or represent Womens partes in the aforesaid Tragedies, Comedies, Playes, or representacions; And in consideration of erectinge and establishinge them to bee a Companie, and his the said Sir William's paines and expences to that purpose for many yeeres. And the other fiue of the said Shares or proporcions is to bee devided amongst the rest of the persons [parties] to theis presentes, whereof the said Henry Harris is to haue an equall share with the greatest proporcions in the said fiue shares or proporcions.

That the generall receiptes of the said Theatre (from and after such time as the said Companie haue performed their playeinge in Salisbury Court, or in any other Playhouse, accordinge to and noe longer then the tyme allowed by him the said William as aforesaid) shall bee by Ballatine, or tickettes soulled[3] for all doores and boxes.

That Sir William Davenant, his Executors, administrators,[4] or assignes, shall at the generall Chardge of the whole Receiptes prouide three persons to receiue money for the said Tickettes,

---

[1] Malone omits "publiquely."
[2] Malone omits "then."
[3] Malone reads "sealed."
[4] Halliwell-Phillipps omits "administrators."

in a roome adioyning to the said Theatre; And that the Actor in the said Theatre, nowe parties to these presents, who are concerned in the said ffive shares or proporcions, shall Dayly or Weekely appoint two or three of themselues, or the men hirelinges deputed by them, to sitt with the aforesaid three persons appointed by him[1] the said Sir William, that they may suruey or giue an accompt of the money receiued for the said Tickettes. That the said seauen shares shalbee paid nightly by the said three persons by the said Sir William deputed, or by anie of them, to him the said Sir William, his Executors, administrators, or assignes.

That the said Sir William Dauenant shall appoint halfe the number of the doorekeepers necessary for the receipt of the said Tickettes for doores and Boxes, the Wardrobe Keeper, barber, and all other necessary persons as hee the said Sir William shall thinke fitt, and their Sallary to bee defrayed at the publique Chardge.

That when any Sharer amongst the Actors of the aforesaid fiue[2] shares, and parties to these presents shall dye, that then the said Sir William Davenant, his Executors, administrators, or assignes, shall haue the denominacion and appointment of the Successor and successors. And likewise that the Wages of the men hirelings shalbee appointed and established by the said Sir William Davenant, his Executors, administrators or assignes.

That the said Sir William Davenant, his executors, administrators, or assignes, shall not bee obliged out of the shares or proporcions allowed to him for the Supplyeinge of Cloathes, Habites, and Scenes, to prouide eyther Hattes, feathers, Gloues, ribbons, sworde belts, bandes, stockinges, or shoes, for any of the men Actors aforesaid, Vnless it be to Properties.[3]

That a priuate boxe bee prouided and established for the vse of Thomas Killigrewe, Esquire, one of the Groomes of his Maiesties Bedchamber, sufficient to conteine sixe persons, into which the said Mister Killigrewe, and such as he shall appoint, shall haue liberty to enter without any Sallery or pay for their entrance into such a place of the said Theatre as the said Sir William Davenant, his heires, Executors, administrators, or assignes shall appoint.

That the said Thomas Batterton, Thomas Sheppey, Robert Noakes, James Noakes, Thomas Louell, John Moseley, Cave Vnderhill, Robert Turner, and Thomas Lilleston, doe hereby for

[1] Malone omits "him."
[2] Malone omits "fiue."
[3] Malone reads "a propertie" instead of "to Properties."

themselues Couenant, promise, graunt and agree, to and with
the said Sir William Davenant, his executors, administrators,
and assignes, by these presentes, That they and euery of them
shall become bound to the said Sir William Dauenant, in a bond
of 5000*li.* condicioned for the performance of these presentes.
And that euery Successor to any part of the said fiue shares or
proporcions shall enter into the like bond before hee or they
shalbe admitted to haue[1] anie part or proporcion of the said
shares or proporcions.

And the said Henry Harris doth hereby for himself, his
Executors, administrators, and assignes, Couenant, promise,
graunte and agree, to and with the said Sir William Dauenaunt,
his Executors, administrators, and assignes, by these presentes,
that hee the said Henry Harris shall within one weeke after
the notice giuen by Sir William Dauenaunt for the Concludinge
of the playeinge at Salisbury Court or any other house else
abouesaid, become bounde to the said Sir William Davenant in
a bond of 5000*li.* condicioned for the performance of these
[presents].[2]   And that euery Successor to any of the said ffiue
shares shall enter into the like bond, before hee or they shalbee
admitted to haue any part or proporcion in the said ffiue shares.

Item, it is mutually agreed by and betweene all the parties to
these presentes, That the said Sir William Dauenant alone shalbee
Master and Superior, and shall from time to time haue the sole
government of the said Thomas Batterton, Thomas Sheppey,
Robert Noakes, James Noakes, Thomas Louell, John Moseley,
Caue Vnderhill, Robert Turner and Thomas Lilleston, and alsoe
of the said Henry Harris, and their Associates, in relacion to the
Playes[3] by these presentes agreed to bee erected.   In Wittness
&c.

Examinatur Cum Originali
Per William Moseley et Ricardum Cwpper.[4]

[1] Malone reads "share."
[2] Malone adds this word in brackets.
[3] Malone in brackets corrects this to "playhouse."
[4] Malone omits the final note in Latin.

## XVI. HERBERT OUTLINES HIS CASE AGAINST THE PLAYERS IN KILLIGREW'S COMPANY[1]

December 1660.          To proue the          and the allowance of          .

To proue the Licensinge of Playhouses and of Playes to Acte.

To proue the suppressinge of Players, and their Obedience.

To proue the allowances made by the Players to my predecessors and my selfe, besides the Fees.

To proue the Lord Chamberlins Grantes & declarations In ayde of the Master of the Reuells.

To produce the Comissions granted to my Predecessors.

To proue my practise by the Grants made by me for 40 yeares to seuerall Companies of Players to Trauell.

To proue the suppressinge of them by warants executed by Constables & Messingers to the King's Chamber.

To proue a sumers day and winters day of cleere proffits allowed by the Company of the Blackfryers, and that they payd 40s. for a new Play & 20s. for reuiuinge of an Olde.

To proue that Mister Beeston payd me 60*li.* per annum besids usuall Fees & allowances for Court plaies.

To proue a share payd by the Fortune Plaiers, and a share by the Bull Plaiers, and a share by Salsbery Court Players.

To produce the Acknowledgments of the Red Bull Actors and of the Cockpit Company.

To produce my Grante.

That the Defendants Acted under the Authority & were hence suppressed by my warants and did not Acte till they had leaue from me.

The Grant under the signet [was made] to Killegrew [and] Dauenant and giues them [the power] to authorize [playes]. It restraenes to the Cities of London & Westminster and [the] Liberties thereof, which cannot be good In law, when the Master of the Reuells Hath tyme out of minde Exercised the powers ouer the Players In allowinge of Plaies, reforminge and orderinge of Players.

And that the present Master of the Reuells doth [authorise] seuerall Companies of Players to trauell In[to] the country and acte by Vertue of Authoritie from the off[ice of the] Reuells

The Authoritie giuen to Killegrew and Dauenant Is not

---

[1] Halliwell-Phillipps, *Collection*, p. 26. Herbert brought action against Mohun and several other members of Killigrew's company in October 1660, and the case was tried in December, 1661.

exclusive to the Master of the Reuells, nor any mention of him therein, so that the Intention of the Grante if good was not to take away any Rights or proffits due to the Master of the Reuells.

## XVII.   CERTIFICATE OF THE DEATH OF ASTLEY[1]

honoured Sir
    A cordin to your desiear I haue sent you a trow sertifiCate of the buryall of Sir John Ashley.

> Sir, I am your faithfull frind
> & searuant to Command,
> William Bickforde.

from maydston the 1. of July, 1661.

Christopher Balldwin, Caryor of maidston, Logeth at the Sine of the pide doge one Saint mary hill nere Billensgate.
ffor the Right Worshipfull Sir henry herbert, thes.

Mister Bukfords Letter [fro]m madstone, with a certificate [of] the deathe of sir John Ashley.   Received the 2 July, 1661.

## XVIII.   BREVIAT, SIR HENRY HERBERT VERSUS SIR WILLIAM DAVENANT[2]

That King Henry 8, by his letters Pattents under the Great Seale of England dated at Westminster the 11th of March in the 36th yeare of his Reigne, did giue and graunt to Thomas Cawardin, Knight, the said Office habendum &c for his life and 10*li*. per Annum fee with power to Constitute a Deputy &c.

> proved by R. Grainge.

That Queen Elizabeth made the like grante to Edmond Tilney, Esquire, 24th July, in the 21th yeare of her Reigne.

> proved by R. Grainge.

That King James made the like Grante to George Buck, Esquire, 21th June, in the first yeare of his Reigne.

> proved by R. Grainge.

---

[1] Halliwell-Phillipps, *Collection*, p. 36.   Herbert probably secured this certificate to use in his suit against Killigrew's company.   Astley died on January 13, 1641.
[2] Halliwell-Phillipps, *Collection*, p. 88; a second copy, with no variations, is also printed by Halliwell-Phillipps.

That King James made the like Grante to John Ashley, Knight, 3. Aprill, in the 10th yeare of his Reigne.

proved by R. Grainge.

That King James made the like grante to Benjamin Johnson, 5. October, in the 19th yeare of his Reigne.

That King Charls the first made the like Grante to Henry Herbert, Knight, and Simon Thelwall, Esquire, 25 August, 5th of his Reigne.

proved by the Grante.

Cook Litt. fol. 115. Crok. 1 part.

A Præscription is the time whereof the memory of man is not to the Contrary, As 60 yeares.

Yong and Steeles case Stat. 9 Eliz. cap. 5.

The words of the Grante Are Officium Magistri Jocorum Reuellorum et Mascorum omnium et singulorum suorum Cum omnibus domibus Mancionibus regardis Proficuis Juribus Libertatibus et Aduantagiis eidem officio quonis modo pertinentibus sive spectare debentibus &c.

New erected mills must pay Tithes, but if a mill was Erected 100 years since so that no man Can prove when. It shall pay no tithes and bee supposed to be erected in Edward 2. time.

It appeares by these words, And by the words of Dedimus et Concessimus et Facimus ordinamus et Constituimus, That at the tyme of the grante by Henry 8 to Cawarden it was not the Creation of the office but the Continuance of it, and that houses profitts &c Could not belong to a new Created office, and that the house the Earle of Elgen now liveth in at Saint Johnes did belong to the office of the Reuells.

A Declaration under William Earle of Pembrokes hand of the Ancjent Powers of the Office 20 Nouember 1622.

That the respectiue masters of the Reuells Successiuely haue Authorized All Showes that Are to be presented by Any Persons in England.

That the defendant prohibited diuers persons from takeing their Authority from the plaintiff, as they ought to do, for Publishing of Shewes, And threatned others and warranted others against the plaintiff, which made them refuse to take their Authority from the plaintiff to the plaintiffs damage

Edward Thomas, John Rogers, John Millard.

That George Harman was by the defendant prohibited to take Any Authority from the Office of the Reuells, And Trauelled into the Country without Any Authority from the office of the Reuells.

Edward Thomas, John Rogers.

That Doctor Lambert was by the defendant prohibited to take an Authority from the Office of the Reuells, And trauelled into the Countrey by Commission from John Pointz.

Edward Thomas, John Rogers.

That the King Cannot grante Away an Incident to an office, though the office bee in the Kings Guift.

1.° Eliza. fol. 175 Dier. Skrogs Case.

That Nicholas Spencer, haueing Authority from the plaintiff, was disturbed by the defendant from exercising his quality by threats and Arrests, and by paying of fiue and Twenty shillinges in money.

See the Authority to Nicholas Spencer.

Sir H. Herbert versus Sir W. Davenant.

## XIX.  BREVIAT, SIR HENRY HERBERT VERSUS SIR WILLIAM DAVENANT [1]

That the Office of the Reuells was Instituted by the Saxons.

ThisGrante was not produced at former tryalls.   Copy proued by R. Grainge.

That Kinge Henry 8. by His Letters Pattents under His Great Seale bearinge date at Westminster the 11. Marche, In the 36. of his Reigne, did give and Grante to Thomas Cawerden, Knight, the said Office Habendum et Exercendum for his Life, and 10*li* ayeare Fee, with power to Constitute a Deputye.

82 years since. Copy proued.

That Queen Elizabeth made the like Grante to Edmond Tilney, Esquire, 24 July, In the 21 yeare of Her Reigne.

Copy proued.

That King James made the like Grante to George Buck, Esquire, 21 June, In the 1 yeare of His Reign.

Copy proued.

That King James made the like Grante to John Ashley, Knight, 3 Aprill, In the 10 yeare of His Reigne.

Copy proued.

That King James made the like Grante to Beniamin Johnson, 5 October, In the 19 yeare of his Reigne.

Great Seale Stat. 9 Elizabeth Cap 5.

That King Charles the first made the like Grante to Henry Herbert, Knight, and to Symon Thelwall, Esquire, for their liues, and the longest liuer of them, 25 August, In the 5 yeare of His Reigne.

[1] Halliwell-Phillipps, *Collection*, p. 91. Herbert brought two actions against Davenant.

The words of the Grant are Officium Magistri Jocorum Revellorum et Mascorum Omnium et singulorum suorum cum Omnibus Domibus Manscionibus Regardis Proficuis Juribus Libertatibus et Aduantagiis eidem Officio quouis modo pertinentibus siue spectantibus uel tali Officio pertinere siue spectare debentibus.

It appeares by these wordes, and by the words of Dedimus et Concessimus et Facimus ordinamus et Constituimus, That It was not the Creation of the Office but the Continuance of it, and that Houses and proffits could not belonge to a New Created office.

That the Allowance of Playes, the Orderinge of Players, and the permittinge of Playhouses Haue tyme out of minde ben In the Exercise and Allowance of the Masters of the Reuells respectiuely.

That the Playes made by Sir William Dauenant, acted at the Blackfryers by the then Kings Company, were allowed for the stage by the Playntiff.

A Grante from King James, dated the 24 February, 17 of His Reigne, to Robert Lea to exercise the Quality of Playinge &c, Prouided that all Authority proffits &c belonginge to the Master of the Reuells shall remaine.

The like Grant made by King Charles first, 7 yeare of His Reigne, To Andrew Caue[1] &c. with the like Prouiso.

A declaration under William Earle of Pembrokes Handes of the Antient powers of the Office, Dated the 20th of Nouember 1622.

Seuerall Plays allowed by Mister Tilney In 1598, which is 62 years since.[2] Sir William Longsword allowed to be Acted the 24 May 1598.
The Faire Mayd of London
And Richard Cordelyon.

Kinge and noe Kinge, to be Acted in 1611, and the same to be printed, Allowed by Sir George Bucke, And Hogg Hath loste His Pearle, by sir George Buck.

That the defendant erected a Company of Players at Salsbery Court, London, the 5th November, 1660, by his owne pretended Authority, and Authorised them to playe Playes, and tooke the

*Marginal notes:*

Newe erected Mills must paye Tythes, but if a mill was erected a 100 yeares agoe so that noe man can proue when erected, it shall paye noe Tythes, and shall be supposed to be Erected In Edward 2 tyme.

Michael Oldsworthe, Richard Hall, William Hall, Rhodes, William Beeston, Sir John Treuor.

See the Grante.

Richard Hall.

see the Articles. proued by Thomas Shippey, William Beeston.

[1] Read "Cane."
[2] See p. 112.

profits &c., In defyance of the Authority of the master of the
Reuells.   As apeares by Articles made betweene the defendant
and Batterton and others &c.[1]

Richard
Hall, William
Hall.

That the Fees payd by the then Kings Company at the Blackfryers about 40 yeares agoe were for a new Playe 40s. for a
reuiued Play 20s. besids other Fees.   And the proffits of a
sumers day and winters day and the like fees from other Companys.

That all sortes of Players actinge In london, Westminster,
or Cuntry, obeyed the Authority of the Playntiff till the defendant set up a new Jurisdiction and protected His pretended
Company against the Playntiff.

1° Elizab.
fo. 175 Dier.
Skrogs Case
Cok. lit. fol.
115 Crok. 1.
part.

That the King cannot grante away an Incident to an Office
thogh the office be In the Kings Guift.

What a good Prescription Is?   The tyme whereof the memory
of man Is not to the Contrairie.   Brac. Lib. 4. fo. 230.

Yonge and Steels Case
Stat. 9. Eliz. Cap. 5.

## XX.   MANDATE OF THE LORD CHAMBERLAINE, JULY 31, 1661, REGARDING THE OFFICE OF THE REVELS AND ITS AUTHORITY[2]

To all Mayors, Sherriffs, Justices of the peace, Bayliffs, Constables, and other his Maiesties Officers, True Leigemen and
Subjects, whom it may concerne, and to every of them: Whereas
I am credibly informed that there are manie and very great
disorders and abuses comitted by divers and sundry companies
of Stage Players, Tumblers, vaulters, dauncers on the Ropes,
and also by such as goe about with motions and Shewes, and
other like kind of persons, by reason of certeyne Grants, Comissions, and Lycenses which they have by secret means procured
from the Kings Maiestie, by vertue whereof they do abusseively
claime unto themselves a kinde of Lycentious freedome to travell
as well to Shew plaie and exercise in Eminent Citties and Cor-
poracions within this Kingdome as alsoe from place to place,
without the Knowledge and Approbacion of his Maiesties office

---

[1] For Herbert's copy of the Articles see Document XV.
[2] Halliwell-Phillipps, *Collection*, p. 42.

of the Revells, and by that means doe take uppon them att there owne pleasure to act and sett forth in many places of this Kingdome divers and sundry plaies and shewes which for the most parte are full of scandall and offence both against the Church and State, and doe likewise greatlie abuse their authoritie in lending, letting, and selling their said Commissions and Lycenses vnto others, By reason whereof divers lawless and wandring persons are suffered to have free passage, unto whom such grants and Lycenses were never intended, Contrary to his Maiesties pleasure, the Lawes of this Land, his Maiesties grant and Commission to the Master of the Revells, and the first institucion of the said Office, Theis are therefore, in his Maiesties name, straightly to charge and command you, and every of you, That whosoever shall repaire to any of your Citties, Borroughs, Townes Corporate, Villages, Hamletts, or parishes, and shall there, by vertue of any Commission, warrant, or Lycence whatsoever, act, sett forth, shew, or present anie Play, Show, Motion, feats of activitie and sights whatsoever; not haveing a Lycense, now in force, under the hand and seale of Office of Sir Henry Herbert, Knight, now Master of his Maiesties office of the Revells, or under the hand of his Deputy, and sealed likewise with the said Seale of the office, That you, and every of you, att all tymes for ever hereafter, doe Seize and take away all and every such grant, pattent, Comission, or Lycence, whatsoever, from the bringer or bearer thereof, and that you fortwith cause the said Graunt or Lycence to be conveyed and sent unto his Maiesties said office of the Revells, there to remaine at the disposicion of the foresaid Master of the said office, And that to the uttermost of your power you doe from henceforth forbidd and suppresse all such Plaies, Shewes, motions, feates of Activitie, sights and every of them, vntill they shall be approved, Lycenced, and authorized by the said Sir Henry Herbert, or his said Deputy, in the manner aforesaid, Who are appointed by his Maiestie under the great Seale of England for that end and purpose; Herein faile you not, as you will answer the contrary at your perrills, And for your more certeintie I advise you to take an exact Coppy of this my Mandate, Given at Whitehall, under my hand and seale, this one and Thirtieth day of July, in the yeare of our Lord God one Thousand six hundred sixty and one.

Manchester

## XXI. DECLARATION, MAY 6, 1662, HERBERT AND THELWALL VERSUS BETTERTON [1]

Sir Henry Herbert, Knight, and Symon Thelwall, Esquire, plaintiffs, and Thomas Betterton defendant in an Accion of the case.

The plaintiffs declare that whereas within this realme of England, to witt at London, in the parish of St. Mary Bowe, in the ward of Cheape, there is, and time out of minde hath been, an office of the Master of the Revells and Masks of our Lord the King, his heires and successors, To which said office, and to which said Master, or Masters, by vertue of that office the licenceing, alloweing, overseing, and correction of all and singuler Comon Actors of Playes and of all stage Playes by them Acted, by the whole time aforesaid haue belonged and apperteined, and doe yett belong and apperteine, for the executing of which said office the Masters of the Revells and Masks aforesaid for the time being from time to time dureing the whole time aforesaid haue had and receiued and haue accustomed to haue and receiue of the Comon Actors of Playes aforesaid for the time being diuers fees, profitts, and emoluments, for the licenceing and allowing the said stage Playes, which said office, togeather with all fees, profitts, and emoluments to the same office belonging and appertening by the whole time aforesaid, was given and graunted and hath been accustomed to be given and graunted by our Lord the King now and his predecessors Kings and Queens of England for the time being to any person or persons willing to exercise the said office: And whereas Queen Elizabeth, by her letters Patents vnder the great seale dated at Westminster, the 24th of July, in the 21th yeare of her Reigne, did graunt the said office to Edmond Tilney, Esquire, habendum the said office to the said Edmond for his life, to be exercised by him or his deputy: By vertue whereof the said Edmond was seized of the said office as of his franktenement for his life, and being soe seized, King James by his letters Patents vnder the great seale the 23th of June in the first year of his Reigne over England, did graunt to George Bucke, then Esquire and afterwards Knight, the said office Habendum the said office to him for his life, to be exercised by himself or his deputy from the time of the death of the said Edmond Tilney, or assoon as the said office should become void by surrender, forfeiture, or other legall manner.   And that afterwards, the 20th of August, 1610, the said Edmond Tilney died,

[1] Halliwell-Phillipps, *Collection*, p. 39.

after whose death the said George Bucke, by vertue of the said graunt of the office, was thereof seized as of his freehold for the terme of his life. And being soe seized, King James, by his Letters Patents vnder the great seale the 3d of April in the 10th year of his Reigne, did graunt the said office to John Ashley, Knight, Habendum to him from the death of the said George Bucke or assoone as the said office by resignacion surrender or other lawfull way should become void for the terme of his life, to be exercised by himselfe or deputy. And whereas alsoe King James, by his other Letters Patents, the 5th of October, in the 19th year of his Reigne, graunted the said office to Beniamin Johnson, gentleman, for his life, from the death of the said George Bucke and John Ashley, or assoon as the said office by resignacion or surrender or other lawfull manner should become void, after which graunt, to witt the 20th of September, 1623, the said George Bucke dyed,[1] after whose death John Ashley, by vertue of the said graunt of the office, was seized thereof as of his freehold for his life. And being soe seized, and the said Beniamin Johnson then alive, the late King Charles, by his Letters Patents vnder the great seale, the 22th of August, in the 5th year of his Reigne, of his certaine knowledge and mere mocion, for himselfe, his heirs and successors, did giue and graunt to the plaintiffs the said office Habendum to them for their liues, and the life of the longer liuer of them after the death of the said John Ashley and Beniamin and assoon as the said office by resignacion, surrender, forfeiture, or other lawfull meanes should become void, with all mancion houses, Regards, profitts, rights, liberties, and advantages to the same office belonging or apperteining. And that afterwards, to witt the 20th of November, 1635, Beniamin Johnson dyed, and on the 13th of January 1640 the said John Ashley dyed, after whose deaths the plaintiffs tooke vpon them the said office, and from thence hitherto haue endeauoured faithfully and diligently to exercise the same, and to haue and receiue the vails fees profitts and advantages to the said office belonging, And that the defendant, intending to hinder the plaintiffs in the vse and exercise of their said office, and to deprive and exclude them of the fees, vailes, regards, profitts, and advantages to the same office belonging, between the 15th of November in the 12th year of the Reigne of our now Lord the King and the day of the bringing the plaintiffs Originall writt, to witt the sixth of May, in the 14th year of this King,

[1] The usual date given is September 22, an error from Chalmers, N. I., p. 203. Malone correctly gives the date, *Variorum*, iii. 181; but on p. 59 he says September 28, obviously a printer's error.

at London, aforesaid, in the parish and ward aforesaid, the said
defendant, with divers others persons, vniustly, and without the
licence or allowance of the said plaintiffs, or either of them, and
against their wills, did Act diuers stage Playes, aswell new Playes
as revived Playes, to witt 10 new playes and 100 revived Playes,
the fees for the licenceing & allowing thereof due to the plaintiffs
or either of them not being paid. And this they lay to their
damage c*li*.

The defendant by Henry Salman his Attorney hath pleaded
not guilty.

Herbert and Thelwall versus Betterton.

Declaration, May 6, 16[62].

## XXII.   BREVIAT, HERBERT AND THELWALL VERSUS BETTERTON[1]

That King Henry 8 by his Letters Pattents under the Great
Seale dated at Westminster the 11th March in the 36th yeare
of his Reigne did giue and grant to Thomas Cawarden, Knight,
the said Office Habendum &c for his life and 10*li*. per Annum
fee, with Power to Constitute a Deputy &c.

proved by R. Grainge.

That Queen Elizabeth made the like Grante to Edmond
Tilney, Esquire, 24. July, in the 21. yeare of her Raigne.

proved by R. Grainge.

That King James made the like Grante to George Buck,
Esquire, 21 June, in the first yeare of his Reigne.

proved by R. Grainge.

---

[1] Halliwell-Phillipps, *Collection*, p. 91. On page 94 Halliwell-Phillipps
prints a "Breviat, Sir Henry Herbert versus Betterton." Since this is merely
a copy of the breviat printed above, I have not reprinted it here. The only
significant difference is the following note jotted down at the end:
    "Not on Record—Sir Richard Guilford.
    36 Henrici—Sir Thomas Cawerden.
    Not on Record—Sir Thomas Benger.
    Not on Record—Sir John Fortescu.
    24 July, Elizabethe 21—Edmund Tilney, Esquire.
    23 June, 1 Jacobi—Sir George Buc.
    10 Jacobi—Sir John Ashley.
    19 Jacobi—Beniamin Johnson.
    25 August, 5 Caroli 1—Sir Henry Herbert and Simon Thelwall, Esquire."

That King James made the like Grante to John Ashley, Knight, 3. Aprill, in the 10th yeare of his Reigne.

proved by R. Grainge.

That King James made the like Grante to Benjamin Johnson, 5 October, in the 19 yeare of his Reigne.

proved by R. Grainge.

That King Charls the first made the like Grant to Henry Herbert, Knight, and Simon Thelwall, Esquire, 25. August. the fifth yeare of his Reign. proved by the Great Seale.

Cook Litt.
ol. 115. Crok
t. Parte.

A Praescription is the time whereof the Memory of man is not to the Contrary, as 60 yeares.

Yong and Steeles Case. Stat. 9. Eliz. Cap. 5

That Sir John Ashley and Benjamin Johnson are dead. proued by Michaell Beauer, Samuell Hooper.

New erect-
ed Mills
must pay
Tithes, but if
a mill was
erected 100
yeares since,
So that no
man can
proue when,
proue when,
t shall pay
noe tithes
and bee sup-
posed to be
erected in
Edward 2ds
ime.

The words of the Grante Are Officium Magistri Jocorum Reuellorum et Mascorum omnium et Singulorum Suorum Cum omnibus Domibus Mancionibus Regardis Proficuis Juribus Libertatibus et Aduantagiis eidem Officio quouis modo pertinentibus siue spectare debentibus &c.

It Appeares by these words, and by the words of Dedimus et Concessimus et Facimus ordinamus et Constituimus, That at the time of the Grant by Henry 8 to Cawarden it was not the Creation of the office but the Continuance of it. And that houses, Profitts, &c. Could not belong to a New Created Office.

That the Allowance of Playes, the Ordering of Players, and Permitting of Playhouses haue time out of minde been in the Exercise and Allowance of the Masters of the Reuells respectiuely.

George Bosgroue Michael Oldsworth Richard Hall William Hall William Beeston Rhodes Sir John Treuor.

That the Playes made by Sir William Dauenant acted at Blackfryers by the then Kings Company were allowed for the stage by the Plaintiff.

A Grante under the Signett from King James, dated 24 February, 17. of his Reigne, to Robert Lea and others to exercise the quality of Playing &c., Prouided that all Authority Profitts &c. due to the Master of the Reuells shall Remaine. see the Grante.

The like Grante made by King Charles the first, 7 yeare of his Reigne, to Andrew Caue[1] and others, with the like Prouiso.

1 Although three breviats spell this "Caue," it is doubtless an error for "Cane," the famous Elizabethan actor.

A Declaration under William Earle of Pembrokes hand of the Ancient Powers of the Office, dated Nouember 20., 1622.

Seuerall Playes Allowed by Mister Tilney in 1598, which is 62 yeares since.[1]
As Sir William Longsword[2] Allowed to bee Acted in 1598.[3]
The Fair Maid of London.[4]
Richard Cordelyon.[5]                                    see the Bookes.

Allowed by Sir George Buck
King and noe King, to bee acted in 1611. and the same to bee Printed.
Hogg hath lost his Pearle,[6] and hundreds more.

Richard Hall.

That the Great house at Saint Johnes's where the Earle of Elgyn liueth did anciently belong to the Office of the Reuells, and was giuen Away by King James to the Lord Aubigny,[7] and an Allowance of fifty pounds a yeare made to the respectiue Masters of the Reuells in lieu of the said house, which to this day is in Charge with the Auditor.

That the defendant Articled with Sir William Dauenant[8] the 5. Nouember 1660 to Acte with the said Dauenant, and under his pretended Authority, at Salsebery Court Playhouse and at the theatre in Portugall Row, to the prejudice of the office of the Reuells and in disturbance of the Priuiledges and Profitts thereof, and to the Plaintiffs Damage.

That All Sortes of Players Acting in London Westminster Suburbs thereof and Countrey obeyed the plaintiffs Authority

---

[1] This passage was printed by Malone, *Var.* iii. 263. It appears also in the Breviat printed on p. 104.

[2] By Michael Drayton, paid for by Henslowe on January 20, 1598-9. Mr. Greg, in his *Commentary* on Henslowe's *Diary*, enters the play as "William Longbeard (?)"; but Drayton himself, in his receipt to Henslowe, spells the word "Longsword," and its reoccurrence in Herbert's note should settle the matter. The play is not extant.

[3] The Breviat printed on p. 104 reads "Allowed to be Acted the 24 May, 1598."

[4] Fleay, *B. C. E. D.* ii. 384, says: "Fair Maid of London, a ballad, S. R. 1597, Jan. 23. No Play." But Herbert's statement "allowed to be acted, 1598" clearly shows that there was a play of that title—possibly the "ballad" entered in S. R., possibly a play on the same subject.

[5] *Richard Coeur-de-lion's Funeral* was written in June, 1598 for Henslowe by Chettle, Drayton, Munday, and Wilson.

[6] By Robert Tailor, acted at Whitefriars in 1613. The Prologue verifies Herbert's note:
> Our long-time rumour'd Hog, so often cross'd
> By unexpected accidents . . . is at length got loose
> Hath a knight's license, and may range at pleasure.

[7] See p. 71.

[8] See p. 96.

till the defendant and others of their Company did joyne with
the said Dauenant to Acte under the said Dauenants pretended
Power, And that the defendant till that time did Acte at the
Cockpitt playhouse under the Plaintiffs Authority, and owned
the same and noe other.

That the King Cannot grante away an Incident to an Office
though the Office bee in the Kings Guift.

1° Elizabeth. fo. 175 Dier. Skrogs Case

Breviat.

Herbert and Thelwall versus Betterton.


## XXIII. ARTICLES OF AGREEMENT BETWEEN HERBERT AND KILLIGREW [1]

Articles of Agreement, Indented, made and agreed vpon, this
fourthe day of June, In the 14. yeare of the Reigne of our
Souueraigne Lord King Charles the second, And In the yeare of
our Lord 1662, Betweene sir Henry Herbert, of Ribsford, In
the County of Worcester, Knight, of the one parte, and Thomas
Killegrew, of Couent Garden, Esquire, on th other Parte, As
followethe:

Imprimis, It is Agreed, That a firme Amity be concluded for
life betweene the said Sir Henry Herbert and the said Thomas
Killegrew.

Item, The said Thomas Killegrew, Esquire, doth for Himselfe
Couenant, promise, grant, and Agree, to paye or cause to be
payd vnto sir Henry Herbert, or to his Assignes, on or before the
fourthe day of August next, All monies due to the said sir Henry
Herbert from the King and Queens Company of Players, called
Mychaell Mohun, William Wintershall, Robert Shaterell, William
Cartwright, Nicholas Burt, Walter Clunn, Charles Hart, and the
rest of that Company, for the new Plaies at fortie shillinges a
Play, and for the Old Reuiued Plaies at twentie shillings a Play
they the said Players Haue Acted since the Eleuenthe of August,
In the yeare of our Lord, 1660.[2]

---

[1] Halliwell-Phillipps, *Collection*, p. 37; Malone, *Var.* iii. 269. Malone
says: "On the back of this paper Sir Henry Herbert has written 'Copy of
the Articles sealed and delivered the 5th June, 62, between Sir H. H. and
Thomas Killegrew. Bonds of 5000/. for the performance of covenants.'"

[2] For a list of these plays see Document XXV, p. 116.

Item, the said Thomas Killegrew, Esquire, doth for Himselfe Couenant, promise, grante, and Agree, to paye or cause to be payd unto the said sir Henry Herbert, or to his Assignes, on or before the fourthe day of August next, such monies as are due to Him for Damages and Costes[1] obteyned at Law against Mychaell Mohun, William Wintershall, Robert Shaterell, William Cartwright, Nicholas Burt, Walter Clunn, and Charles Hart, upon An Action of the Case brought by the said sir Henry Herbert In the Courte of Comon Pleas against the said Mychaell Mohun, William Wintershall, Robert Shatterell, William Cartwright, Nicholas Burt, Walter Clunn, and Charles Hart, whereupon a Uerdict Hath ben obtayned as aforesaid against them. And Likewise doe promise and Agree that the Costes and charges of suite upon another Action of the Case brought by the said sir Henry Herbert, against the said Mychaell Mohun and the rest of the Players aboue named, shall be also payd to the said sir Henry Herbert or to His Assignes, on or before the fourthe[2] day of August next.[3]

Item, the said Thomas Killegrew, Esquire, doth for Himselfe Couenant, promise, grante, and Agree, that the said Mychaell Mohun and the rest of the Kings and Queenes Company of Players shall, on or before the said fourthe day of August next, paye or cause to be payd vnto the said sir Henry Herbert, or to His Assignes, the sume of fiftie pounds, As a noble[4] present from them, for His great[5] damages susteyned from them and by their means.

Item, That the said Thomas Killegrew, Esquire, doth Couenant, promise, gr[ante, and] Agree, to be aydinge and Assistinge unto the said sir Henry Herbert [in the] due Execution of the office of the Reuells, and neither directly nor Indirectly to Ayde or Assiste sir William Dauenante, Knight, or a[ny of] His pretended Company of Players, or any other Company of Play[ers] to be raysed by Him, or any other Company of Players[6] whatsoever, In the due Execution of the said office as aforesaide, soe as the ayd for[7] to bee required of the said Thomas Killegrew extend vnto[8] the silencing or oppressions of the said King and Queenes Company.

[1] Malone prints "losses."
[2] "The said fourthe," Malone.
[3] For Killigrew's "promise" see the next document, p. 115.
[4] Malone omits the word "noble."
[5] Malone omits the word "great."
[6] Malone omits "to be raysed by Him or any other Company of Players."
[7] Malone reads "soe."
[8] Malone reads "not to."

And the said sir Henry Herbert doth for Himselfe Couenant, promise, grant, and Agree, not to molest the said Thomas Killegrew, Esquire, or His Heirs, In any suite at Lawe or otherwise, to the preiudice of the Grante made unto him by His Maiestie, or to Disturbe the Receiuinge of the proffits arysing by Contract from the Kings and Queens Company of Players to Him, but to ayde and Assiste the said Thomas Killegrew, In the d[ue] Execution of the legall powers granted unto him by His Maiestie f[or the] orderinge of the said Company of Players, and In the leuyinge and Receiuinge of the monies due to Him the said Thomas Killegrew, Esquire, or which shall be due to Him from the saide Company of Players by Any Contract made or to be made between them Concerninge[1] the same, and neither directly nor Indirectly to Hinder the payment of the said monies to be made weekly or otherwise by the said Company of Players to the said Thomas Killegrew, Esquire, or to His Assignes, but to be aydinge and Assistinge to the said Thomas Killegrew, Esquire, And His Assignes therein, if there be cause for it, and that the said Thomas Killegrew desire it of the said sir Henry Herbert.

And the said sir Henry Herbert doth for Himselfe Couenant, promise, grante, and Agree, upon the performance of the matters which are Herein contayned, and to be performed by the said Thomas Killegrew, Accordinge to the daies of payment, and other things Lymited and Expressed in these Articles, to deliuer Into the Handes of the said Thomas Killegrew the Deede of Couenantes, sealed and deliuered by the said Mychaell Mohun and the others Herein named, bearinge date the 11. August, 1660; To be cancelled by the said Thomas Killegrew, or Kept, as He shall thinke fitt, or to make what further Aduantage of the same In my Name or Right as He shall be aduised.

## XXIV. KILLIGREW'S PROMISE TO PAY THE COSTS OF HERBERT'S SUIT AGAINST THE PLAYERS[2]

*Mr. Killegrewe's Promise to pay the Costes of Suite against the Players.*

Julley 14, 1662

I, Thomas Killigrew, doe by this presentes obleige myselfe to paey to Sir Henry Herbert all the costes and charges he shall

---

[1] Malone reads "or amongst."
[2] Rebecca Warner, *Epistolary Curiosities*, Appendix, No. 4, p. 184. This should be read in connection with the preceding document.

ap , othe make apear, to be expendded in the sute betwixt him and the Kinges companye of acters, in the axion of the caes which he had a werdict for against them, in Ield Hall, woen [owing]; and a part thereof, fortey pound, I hafe paid him. Witness my hande and seale the day and date over saide,

THO. KILLIGREWE.

*Witness,*
  Jo. Carew,
  L. Kirke,
  Walter Gyles.


## XXV. PLAYS ACTED BY THE KING'S COMPANY
### 1600–1662 [1]

Nouember '60.  This is a List of plays acted by the Kings Companie at the Red Bull and the new house in Gibbon's Tennis Court near Clare Market.[2]

| | |
|---|---|
| Monday the 5. Nouember. '60. | Wit without money. |
| Tusday the 6. No. | The Traitor. |
| Wensday the 7. No. | The Beggers Bushe. |
| Thursday the 8 No. | Henry the fourthe. First Play. Acted at the new Theatre. |
| Friday the 9. No. | The merry wifes of Windsor. |
| Saterday the 10. No. | The sylent Woman. |
| Monday the 12. No. | [Loues Mistery.] [3] |
| Tusday the 13. No. | Loue lies a Bleedinge. |
| Wensday the 14. No. | |
| Thursday the 15. No. | Loues Cruelty. |
| Friday the 16. No. | The widowe. |
| Saterday the 17. No. | The mayds Tragedy. |
| monday the 19. No. | The Unfortunate Louers. |
| Tusday the 20. No. | The Beggars Bushe. |
| Wensday the 21. No. | The Scornfull Lady. |
| Thursday the 22. No. | The Trayter. |
| Friday the 23. No. | The Elder Brother. |
| Saterday the 24. No. | The Chances. |

[1] Halliwell-Phillipps, *Collection*, p. 34; Malone, *Var.* iii. 273.  This list was prepared, it seems, to exact payment from the King's Company, as promised by Killigrew; see Document XXIII, p. 113.
[2] In the MS. this is written as a marginal note.  For an account of the King's Company and their plays see Downe's *Roscius Anglicanus*.
[3] Erased in the original.  Not included by Malone.

| | |
|---|---|
| Monday the 26. No. | The Opertunity. |
| Tusday the 27. No. | |
| Wensday the 28. No. | |
| Thursday the 29. No. | The Humorous Lieutenant. |
| Friday the 30. No. | |
| Saterday the 1. De. | Claricilla. |
| Monday the 3. De. | A Kinge and no Kinge. |
| Tusday the 4. De. | |
| Wensday the 5. De. | |
| Thursday the 6. De. | Rollo, Duke of Normandy.● |
| Friday the 7. De. | |
| Saterday the 8. De. | The moore of Venice. |
| Monday the 9. Jan. | The weddinge. |
| Saterday the 19. Jan. | The Lost Lady. |
| Thursday the 31. Jan. | Argalus and Parthenia. |
| | |
| | Loyall Subject.[1] |
| | Mad louer. |
| | The wildgoose chase. |
| | All's Loste by Luste. |
| March. 61. | The mayde In the mill. |
| Aprill | A wife for a monthe. |
| May | The bondman. |
| July | |
| Aug. | |
| Sept. | |
| Oct. | |
| Nouemb. | |

| | |
|---|---|
| The Dancinge Master.[2] | |
| Uittoria Corumbana. | 11. [Decemb.] |
| The Cuntry Captaine. | 13. [Decemb.] |
| The Alchymist. | 16. Decemb. |
| Bartholomew Faire. | 18. Decemb.[3] |

[1] Malone says "Between Argalus and Parthenia and the Loyal Subject he has drawn a line." I give below Malone's (1790) reading of the next twelve lines:

| | |
|---|---|
| Feb. | Loyal Subject. |
| | Mad Lover. |
| | The Wild-goose Chase |
| 1661. March ⎫ | All's Loste by Luste |
| April ⎬ . . . . | The Mayd in the Mill |
| May ⎭ | A Wife for a Monthe. |
| | The Bondman |

[2] Malone adds the date "Decemb. 10."
[3] Malone gives the date as "Decemb. 17."

|  |  |  |
|---|---|---|
|  | The Spanishe Curate. | 20. Decemb. |
|  | The Tamer Tamed. | 23. De. |
|  | Aglaura. | 28. De. |
|  | Bussy Dambois. | 30. De. |
|  | mery deuill of Edmonton. | 6. Janu[ary]. |
|  | The Uirgin martire. | 10. Jan. |
|  | Philaster. | 11. Jan. |
|  | Jouiall Crew. | 21. Jan. |
|  | Rule a wife and Haue a wife. | 28. Jan. |
|  | Kinge and noe Kinge. | 15. Febr. |
|  | The mayds Tragedy. | 25. Febr. |
|  | Aglavara the Tragicall way. | 27. Febr.[1] |
|  | Humorous Lieutenant. | 1. March..62. |
| A new Play. | Zelindra. | 3. March. |
|  | The Frenche dancinge Master. | 11. March. |
|  | The Litle Theefe. | 15. March. |
|  | northerne Lasse. | 4. Aprill. |
|  | Fathers owne son. | 19. Aprill. |
| new Play | The Surprizall. | 23. Aprill.[2] |
|  | Knight of the Burninge Pestle. | 5. May. |
| Sir J. Sucklings | Brenoralt. | 12. May. |
|  | Loue In a maze. | 17. May. |
|  |  | June. |
|  |  | July. |
|  | Loues Mistres. | 26 Oct. 61. |
|  | Contented Collinell.[3] |  |
|  | Loue at first sight. |  |
| June 1. 62. | Cornelia a New Play, sir W. Bartleys. |  |
| June 6. 62. | Renegado. |  |
| July 6. 62. | The Brothers. |  |
|  | The Antipodes. |  |
| July 23. 62. | The Cardinal. |  |

[1] From this point to the end, the plays are misplaced by Halliwell-Phillipps, who prints them at the beginning, before the title. Apparently these were on a single sheet of paper which was accidentally misplaced. I have followed Malone's order.

[2] Malone gives the date as "April 25."

[3] Malone corrects to "Discontented Colonel," the second title of Suckling's *Brennoralt*. Opposite he gives the year "1661"; this, however, seems to be a printer's blunder.

## XXVI. DAVENANT'S PETITION AGAINST HERBERT [1]

To the King's most Sacred Majesty.

The humble Petition of Sir William Davenant, Knight, Sheweth,

That your Petitioner has bin molested by Sir Henry Harbert with severall prosecutions at Law.

That those prosecutions have not proceeded by your Petitioners default of not paying the said Henry Harbert his pretended Fees, (he never having sent for any to your Petitioner,) but because your Petitioner hath publiquely presented Plaies; notwithstanding he is authoriz'd therevnto by Pattent from your Majesties most royall Father, and by severall Warrants vnder your Majesties royal hand and signet.[2]

That your Petitioner (to prevent being out Lawd) has bin enforc'd to answer him in Two Tryals at Law, in one of which, at Westminster, your Petitioner hath had a Verdict against him, where it was declar'd that he hath no Jurisdiction over any Plaiers, nor any right to demand Fees of them. In the other, (by a Londen Jury,) the master of Revels was allow'd the correction of Plaies, and Fees for soe doeing; but not to give Plaiers any licence or authoritie to play, it being prov'd that no Plaiers were ever authoriz'd in London or Westminster, to play by the Commission of the Master of Revels, but by authoritie immediately from the Crowne. Neither was the proportion of Fees then determind, or made certaine; because severall witnesses affirm'd that Variety of paymentes had bin made; sometimes of a Noble, sometimes of Twenty, and afterwards of Forty shillings, for correcting a new Play; and that it was the custome to pay nothing for supervising reviv'd Plaies.

That without any authoritie given him by that last Verdict, he sent the day after the tryall a prohibition under his hand and seale (directed to the Plaiers in Litle Lincolnes Inn fields) to forbid them to act Plaies any more.

Therefore your Petitioner humbly praies that your Majesty will graciously please (Two Verdicts having pass'd at Common Law contradicting each other) to referre the Case to the examination of such honourable persons as may certify[3] your Majesty of the just authoritie of the Master of Revells, that so his Fees, (if any be due to him) may be made certaine, to prevent extor-

---

[1] Halliwell-Phillipps, *Collection*, p. 48; Malone, *Var.* iii. 263.
[2] See Adams, *Shakespearean Playhouses*, pp. 424–31.
[3] Malone reads "satisfy."

sion; and time prescrib'd how long he shall keep plaies in his hands, in pretence of correcting them; and whether he can demand Fees for reviv'd Plaies; and lastly, how long Plaies may be layd asyde, ere he shall judge them to be reviv'd.

And your Petitioner (as in duty bound) shall ever pray, &c.

## XXVII. DAVENANT'S PETITION REFERRED TO THE LORD HIGH CHANCELLOR AND THE LORD CHAMBERLAIN [1]

At the Court at Hampton Court, the 30th of June, 1662.

His Majesty, being graciously inclind to have a just and friendly agreement made betweene the Petitioner and the said Sir Henry Harbert, is pleas'd to referre this Peticion to the right honorable the Lord high Chancellor of England, and the Lord Chamberlaine, who are to call before them, aswell the Petitioner, as the said Sir Henry Harbert, and upon hearing and examining their differences, are to make a faire and amicable accommodation between them, if it may be, or otherwise to certify his Majesty the true state of this business, together with their Lordships' opinions.

EDWARD NICHOLAS.

Wee appoint Wednesday morning next before Tenn of the Clock to heare this businesse, of which Sir Henry Harbert and the other Parties concern'd are to have notice, my Lord Chamberlaine having agreed to that hower.

July 7, 1662.                                      CLARENDONE.

## XXVIII. HERBERT'S REPLY TO DAVENANT'S PETITION [2]

To the R$^t$. Honn.$^{rble}$ Edward Earle of Clarendon, Lord High Chancellor of England, and Edward Earle of Manchester, Lord Chamberlain of his M.$^{ties}$ Household.

[1] Halliwell-Phillipps, *Collection*, p. 49; Malone, *Var.* iii. 265.
[2] Not in Halliwell-Phillipps, *Collection*. Malone, who prints it in *Var.* iii. 266, introduces it thus: "On the reference to the Lord Chancellor and Lord Chamberlain, Sir Henry Herbert presented the following statement of his claims."

In obedience to your lordships commandes signifyed unto mee on the ninth of this instant July, do make a remembrance of the fees, profittes, and incidents, belongeinge to y<sup>e</sup> office of the Reuells. They are as followeth:

| | £ | s. | d. |
|---|---|---|---|
| For a new play, to bee brought with the booke........................ | 002 | 00 | 00 |
| For an old play, to be brought with the booke........................ | 001 | 00 | 00 |
| For Christmasse fee................ | 003 | 00 | 00 |
| For Lent fee....................... | 003 | 00 | 00 |
| The profittes of a summers day play at the Blackfryers, valued at........ | 050 | 00 | 00 |
| The profitts of a winters day, at Black-fryers........................ | 050 | 00 | 00 |
| Besides seuerall occasionall gratuityes from the late K<sup>s</sup>. company at B. fryers | | | |
| For a share from each company of four companyes of players (besides the late Kinges Company) valued at a 100*l*. a yeare, one yeare with another, besides the usuall fees, by the yeare........ | 400 | 00 | 00 |
| That the Kinges Company of players couenanted the 11th of August, 60, to pay Sir Henry Herbert per week, from that tyme, aboue the usual fees...... | 004 | 00 | 00 |
| That Mr. William Beeston couenanted to pay weekly to Sir Henry Herbert the summe of................ | 004 | 00 | 00 |
| That Mr. Rhodes promised the like per weeke...................... | 004 | 00 | 00 |

That the 12*l*. per weeke from the three forenamed companyes hath been totally deteyned from Sir Henry Herbert since the said 11<sup>th</sup> Aug. 60, by illegal and unjust means; and all usual fees, and obedience due to the office of the Revells.

That Mr. Thomas Killigrew drawes 19*l*. 6*s*. per week from the Kinges Company, as credibly informed.

That Sir William Dauenant drawes 10 shares of 15 shares, which is valued at 200*l*. per week, cleer profitt, one week with another, as credibly informed.

Allowance for charges of suites at law, for that Sir Henry Herbert is unjustly putt out of possession and profittes, and could not obtaine an appearance gratis.

Allowance for damages susteyned in creditt and profittes for about two yeares since his Ma.^{ties} happy Restauration.

Allowance for their New Theatre to bee used as a playhouse.

Allowance for new and old playes acted by Sir William Dauenantes pretended company of players at Salisbury Court, the Cockpitt, and now at Portugall Rowe, from the 5th Novemb. 60. the tyme of their first conjunction with Sir William Dauenant.

Allowance for the fees at Christmasse and at Lent from the said tyme.

A boxe for the Master of the Reuells and his company, gratis; —as accustomed.

A submission to the authority of the Revells for the future, and that noe playes, new or old, bee acted, till they are allowed by the Master of the Reuells.

That rehearsall of plays to be acted at court, be made, as hath been accustomed, before the Master of the Reuells, or allowance for them.

Wherefore it is humbly pray'd that delay being the said Dauenants best plea, wh^{ch} he hath exercised by illegal actinges for almost two yeares, he may noe longer keep Sir Henry Herbert out of possession of his rightes; but that your Lordshippes would speedily assert the rights due to the Master of the Reuells, and ascertaine his fees and damages, and order obedience and payment accordingly. And in case of disobedience by the said Dauenant and his pretended company of players, that Sir Henry Herbert may bee at liberty to pursue his course at law, in confidence that he shall have the benefitt of his Ma.^{tys} justice, as of your Lordshippes fauour and promises in satisfaction, or liberty to proceed at law. And it may bee of ill consequence that Sir Henry Herbert, dating for 45 yeares meniall service to the Royal Family, and hauing purchased Sir John Ashley's interest in the said office, and obtained of the late Kings bounty a grante under the greate seale of England for two liues, should have noe other compensation for his many yeares faithfull services, and constant adherence to his Ma.^{tys} interest, accompanyed with his great sufferinges and losses, then to bee ousted of his just posseesion, rightes and profittes, by Sir William Dauenant, a person who exercised the office of Master of the Reuells to Oliuer the Tyrant, and wrote the First and Second Parte of Peru, acted at the Cockpitt, in Oliuers tyme, and soly in his fauour; wherein hee sett of the justice of Oliuers actinges, by comparison with the Spaniards, and endeavoured thereby to make Oliuers crueltyes appeare mercyes, in respect of the Spanish crueltyes; but the mercyes of the wicked are cruell.

That the said Dauenant published a poem in vindication and justification of Oliuers actions and government, and an Epithalamium in praise of Olivers daughter M*. Rich; —as credibly informed.

The matters of difference betweene Mr. Thomas Killegrew and Sir Henry Herbert are upon accomodation.

My Lordes,
Your Lordshippes very humble Servant,

HENRY HERBERT.

July 11th 62.
Cary-house.


## XXIX. HERBERT'S LOSSES[1]

Sir Henry Herbert, Knight, Master of his Maiesties office of the Revells by Grant under the greate Seale 5 Caroli Primi Hath time out of minde whereof the memory of man is not to the Contrary, As soly belonging and properly apertaininge to the said office of the Revells; the Allowance of all playes in England and the ordering and performing of all players and the ffees and profitts arysing thereby and hath receiued seuerall ffees and profitts from the said players that doe now Act for a Certaine time, but of Late the said players doe refuse to pay the said fees and profitts formerly payd and due to the said office and haue totally with drawne the payment of them to Sir Henry Herberts damage of fiue thousand pounds.


## XXX. ORDERS FOR THE FAIR AT BRISTOL[2]

Instructions to Edward Thomas, one of the Messengers belonging to his Maiesties office of the Revells, xxiii[th] of July 1663.

1. You are forthwith to make your repaire to the Citie of Bristoll (the ffaires approaching) and soe soone as you come thither, acquaint the Maior of the said Citie, with his Maiesties Grants to vs, and the Lord Chamberleines mandate, touching musick, Cockfightings, maskings, prizes, Stage players, tumblers,

---

[1] Halliwell-Phillipps, *Collection*, p. 45. No date is given for this document; but clearly it relates to the losses sustained by Herbert through the grant to Killigrew and Davenant.
[2] Halliwell-Phillipps, *Collection*, p. 50.

vaulters, dancers on the ropes, such as act, sett forth, shew or present any play, shew, motion, feats of actiuity, or sights whatsoever; as also the authoritie you haue from this office;

2. You are to enquire out the names of all such persons, as are come, or shall come to the said Citie during the time of the faire, with an intention to present any of the things abouementiond, and having found the Master, or cheife person of each company, to demand his Commission, and in case hee hath any vnder the seale of this office, and the time not expired, then you are to suffer him to proceed, after you haue taken notice when the said Commission did commence and determine; But if you find any (as noe doubt you will) who haue not authority from this office, to act as aforesaid, you are to acquaint the cheife Magistrate with it, that all such persons may bee suppressed, and kept in safe custody by you, vntill they shall become bound, with good security to the master of his Maiesties office of the Revells, to appeare at this office within ten daies after such apprehension, vpon the penaltie of twentie Pounds, to answere their contempt, and if they haue not by their obstinacy or abuse forfeited the fauour of the office, to receive respectiue Commissions for their future acting, and to bee Limitted, that they doe nothing thereby offensiue against the Lawes of God or the Land.

3ly. Notwithstanding the premisses, if you find any persons there, which are Inhabitants in Wales, or other remote places, who seldome or never come to London, and without very great preiudice cannot attend the office, you are to permitt them for the fairetime onely, provided they keepe good rule, and pay a present acknowledgement to the office, which you are to receiue, and become engaged in a bond of twenty pounds, to the master of his Maiesties office of the Revells, that they will not act or shew any more without Lycence from the said office either there or in any other place.

4ly. and lastly, you are required soe to order your busines as to render a punctuall accompt in writing at your returne to London, as to each particular contained in these instruccions, or what els may bee omitted through hast, as Mountebankes, Lotteries or the like relating in any kind to the office of the Revells, And this shall warrant your soe doing. Given vnder our hands and seales, at his Maiesties office of the Revels.

E. Hayward.[1]

J. Poyntz.[2]

23th July 1663. Instruccions to Edward Thomas in order to his journey to Bristoll

[1] Herbert's deputy.
[2] The Deputy Clerk Comptroller.

## XXXI. THE MASTER OF THE REVELS AND THE PRESS [1]

**25th July 1663.** Arguments to proue that the Master of his Maiesties Office of the Revells, hath not onely the power of Lycencing all playes, Poems, and ballads, but of appointing them to the Press.

That the Master of his Maiestie's office of the Revells, hath the power of Lycencing all playes whether Tragedies, or Comedies before they can bee acted, is without dispute and the designe is, that all prophanenes, oathes, ribaldry, and matters reflecting vpon piety, and the present gouernement may bee obliterated, before there bee any action in a publique Theatre.

The like equitie there is, that all Ballads, songs and poems of that nature, should pass the same examination, being argued a Majore ad Minus, and requiring the same antidote, because such things presently fly all over the Kingdome, to the Debauching and poisoning the younger sort of people, vnles corrected, and regulated.

The like may bee said as to all Billes for Shewes, and stage playes, Mountebankes, Lotteries &c. because they all receive Commissions from the Master of the Revells who ought to inspect the same, that their pretences may agree with what is granted by their Commissions, otherwise many of them may Divide their Companies and by way of cheat (as hath beene vsuall) make one Commission serve for two Companies, if not for three.

Now from the premisses, it may bee concluded but rationall, that hee who hath the power of allowing and Lycencing (as the Master hath) should likewise bee authorised to appoint and order the press, least after such examination and allowance, alterations should bee made, and the abuse proue a scandall and reflection vpon the Master, and therefore all sober, considerate persons must from the premisses conclude, that the ordering of the Press doth of right belong to the Master of the Revells; and in order to the regulating of this business, and to make it knowne to the world, that not onely the power of it, but the care of well ordering, bounding and correcting

---

[1] Halliwell-Phillipps, *Collection*, p. 51. The British Museum Catalogue, Add. MSS. 19256, says that this document is in the handwriting of Edward Hayward.

all vnsauoury words, and vnbecomming expressions, (not fitt to bee Lycenced in a christian Commonwealth,) belongeth solely and properly to the Master of the Revells, all Poetts and Printers, and other persons concerned, are to take notice, after this manifestation shall come out, or a precept Drawne from thence, bee sent vnto them that they and every of them doe for the future, forbeare their poetry and printing, soe farre as may concerne the premisses, without Lycence first obteined from the Office of the Revells, over against Petty Cannons hall in St. Pauls churchyard, where they may certainely find one or more of the officers every day.

25th July. 1663.   Arguments to proue that the Master of his Maiesties Office of the Revells, hath not onely the power of Lycenceing all Playes, poems and ballads, but of appointing them to the Press.

## XXXII.  INFORMATION DESIRED BY EDWARD HAYWARD, HERBERT'S DEPUTY[1]

27th July 1663.   Remembrances when I waite vpon Sir Henry Herbert.

1. To call vpon him for the Records, which hee promised, having asyet onely half a dozen loose Presidents.
2. To desire him to appoint a time for the making of mee knowne to the lord Chamberleine, Sir William Davenant, Mister Killegrew, Sir Edward Griffin, Threasurer of the Chamber, and the Lord Chamberleines Secretaries, that in Sir Henry's absence I may haue free access to them either personally or by letters.
3. To know of Sir Henry what Dutie or attendance is required of mee at Whitehall, that I may not bee wanting therein, and charged with neglect, when time shall come to Demand my quarterly allowances and Wages, and likewise to know from whom it is to be paid and the times when.
4. To bee informed what allowances Captain Poyntz can by ancient or moderne custome Demand, as Clerks Comptroller and Clerk over and aboue the rates and fees sett Downe by Sir Henry Herbert as the Master's Fees, and what Captain Poyntz his Dutie is as to such demands and what the opinion of Councell

[1] Halliwell-Phillipps, *Collection*, p. 53.

hath beene, at the close of contests betweene Sir Henry and him, and whether Sir Henry did ever waue any of his trialls, out of a feare or Doubtfulnes of being cast.

5. To be informed by Sir Henry, whether it Doth not as equally belong to him to Lycence all Poems and Ballads as play bookes, which I may not omitt to enquire after, for the enlarging and extending of my profitts, if the thing in it self proue feasable, and it wilbe the better for Sir Henry, if hee survive mee, for I intend to make a Diligent enquiry after the rights of the Office, and to contend soberly and cautiously for them:

6. To bee informed whether it may bee prudentiall and safe to make vse of Mister Rogers and his Soldiers, vpon any private accompt saue at Bartholemew faire, and other faires within the Cities of London and Westminster, and the liberties thereof.

7. To know of Sir Henry Herbert, what playes haue beene Lycenced or allowed vpon since the 11th of this instant July.

8. To know what is Done about Mister Pagett, and whether it bee necessary for mee to attend the Lord Chamberleine about it.

9. To enquire whether Sir Henry did not (as a branch of his office), sometimes lycence Billiard tables Nine pinnes, &c. and what fee hee vsually tooke for the same, what president or footsteps there was for it, and why hee Declined it.

10. Whether particular musitians are not to bee lycenced aswell as companies, for that if they bee left free, they may gather into companies without a Commission, and the Master may loose his fees.

11. Whether new playes or reviu'd playes being once lycenced, shall pay noe further Duties to the Master my meaning is, what duration of time, brings either of them within the compass of a new allowance by the Master.

12. To know how farre I may proceed (quasi Masters Deputy) against such as shall not render themselves vpon summons, or warrants whereby they may bee reduced to an obedience and conformitie to the Master's iust commands, my Designe is to avoid too frequent troubling of my Lord Chamberleine, vnles in extraordinary cases.

13. To entreat soe much fauor from Sir Henry, as that his Clerke may search the bookes, and informe mee what numbers of the severall companies vnderwritten are in England, and how many of them by name are out of Commission, and when, because none haue as yet appeared. Viz$^t$.

Mountebankes
Lotteries

Clockwork mocions
Ordinary motions
extra motions
Dancing horses and mares
Ropedancers
Slights of hand.

14. To know if I haue not the priuiledge of a box in each playhouse, being told that Sir Henry had one at Command when hee pleased, for himself or friends.

15. To bee informed whether Captain Poyntz hath the Like, or any priuiledge at all, as Clerk Comptroller and clerk, because hee affirmes soe much in many respects and resolues to contend for them.

16. To know how to blazon Sir Henryes coat of armes, and what the Crest is, because I intend to haue it in the office out of respect to him vnder whom I act.

To know whether Cockfighting, belongs not to the Master of the Revells.

17. To propound vnto Sir Hnery the willingnes of Captain Poyntz (that all former Differences may bee buried in oblivion) to giue a generall release to Sir Henry, and the like is Desired from Sir Henry to him.

18. To enquire of Sir Henry, whether the vestures belonging to the severall stageplayers, are not to be provided by the Master of the Revells, for that some records with Captain Poyntz, which were Mister Walkers and others concernd in King James his time, doe manifest soemuch.

Memorandum old Mister Whitehead affirmes, that all Comedies, Tragedies, Poems, Ballads, half sides, drolleries, and all billes relating to Jokes belongs to the Revells, & were soe accompted in the times of Queen Elizabeth and King James, and furthe ¡sayes that to his knowledge Edward Walker formerly servant to Sir Henry tooke moneyes for concealing many of the particulars Last mentioned.

19. To desire of Sir Henry Herbert a copie of the articles betweene him and Mister Killigrew, that I may know what further to expect, and because it is reported, that great matters are to bee expected from the Duke of Yorks playhouse, I desire to know what that may probably bee.

Remembrances when I Waite vpon Sir Henry Herbert.

Memorandum, to desire a copie of Sir Henryes Patent.

———————

Honourd Sir

I came this day purposely to waite vpon you and to dine with you that I might take your advice as to many particulars, and was vnwilling to trouble you before now, by reason of your much attendance at the parliament house. But being come in vaine I made bold to transmitt the enclosed, and to beg your resolucion in the margent to each particular therein mentioned, and to returne it by the first safe opportunity, for till then I resolue not to close with Captain Poyntz; but to keepe my distance as I haue done hitherto, and to preserve the reputacion of the master in myselfe, if I may receiue countenance.

Another paper of my owne drafting, I haue made bold also to send, craving your advice in it, I see I must vse my witts in an honest way or els I shall fall much short of my expectacion, and therefore beg your concurrent helpe and advice.

Thus wishing you a good journey and safe returne.

I remaine, honourd Sir,

Your most humble servant,

E. HAYWARD.

Lincolne house 28th July, 1663.

To the right worshipfull Sir Henry Herbert, Knight, at Ribsford, neere Bewdley, in Worcestershire, these humbly present.

## XXXIII. THE ACCOUNTS OF THE REVELS [1]

The Office Master of Revells.

The Accomptantes Leidgerbookes to bee Signed by the Comptroller, Clerke, and Yeoman of the Revells, aswell as the Master, accordinge to the Course of the office.

A dormant warrant of the Lord Threasurer or Chancellour of the Exchequer for 50*li*. per annum Rent of the Masters howse and office wanting.

The like for 15*li*. per annum for Rent of a howse for the Clerke of the Revells.

The like for 15*li*. per annum for Rent of a howse for the Yeoman of the Revells.

Order of the Lord Chamberlaine for Extraordinary Allowances to the Officers of the Revells at xxiii*li*. xiii*s*. iii*d*. per annum wanting.

[1] Halliwell-Phillipps, *Collection*, p. 84.

Query what shalbee allowed for the fees of the Clerkes of the Signett and Privy Seale and Officers of the Receipt the Accomptant demands x*li.* per annum.

The Master and the rest of the Officers of the Revells theire patents not yet produced.

Revells.    From Auditor Beale.

There hath bin 20*li.* formerly allowed for 3 years. Now there is 10*li.* demanded yearely.

## XXXIV. JOHN POYNTZ TO SIR HENRY HERBERT[1]

Sir Henry

I make bold by theis lines to acquaint your Worshipp That on Tuesday last I Was summoned before the Kings Majesty and Counsell by Sir Richard Hubbard, who accused me there with officiating the Masters office of the Revells and licenceing of Games to his great prejudice. To which I pleaded, that the right of Licecencing [*sic*] of all manner of Games and playes did belonge to your pattent, Wherevpon his Majesty being present did Comand that neither Sir Richard Hubbard nor your deputy should licence any manner of Games for the future. Mister Hayward not being sumoned as I was, would not appeare; wherefore I am very Jealous he will loose that branch of your Pattent for want of pleading: Therefore beseech you stand in the Gapp and vse some meanes by letters to the Lord Chamberlaine who is your Worshipp's great freind in this Case, and he is displeased with Sir Richard Hubbard for bringing a matter before the Counsell, that he is only Judge of, (the Law excepted). I very much feare wee shall be much streightned in payeing the yearely Sallary to you except you helpe vs in this matter: This favour I begg of you, that you will please to approve and allowe of the Method that I have formerly given vnder my hand as Concerning Gameing, of which I have sent your Worshipp a blancke.[2] I did with Mister Hayward give the same with his Licence, but before the time of Mister Hayward I did assume it alone, And therefore hope now you will rather Ratify and Confirme what I did formerly, seeing that I am at present Complying with him who is your Deputy; I begg your favour herein, if possibly it may be obteined of you. One favour more I begg of you, that you would obliviate all differencies and provocacions that I

---

[1] Halliwell-Phillipps, *Collection*, p. 57. Poyntz was the Deputy Clerk Comptroller of the Revels.
[2] See the next document, p. 131.

have given you. And that your Worshipp would be pleased to send vs the heads of every officers duty, That wee May bring in moneys into the said office to pay you from time to time as it growes due. Pardon me that I make this offer to your Worshipp of giveing you a generall Release, I desire heartily to doe it, and begg the favour that your Worshipp will sende me the same. So begging your favour not to take exceptions for what I have writt, With my humble service presented to your Selfe and all yours in generalle.

I Remaine Your dutifull humble and obliged Servant to Comaund to my power till death seperates

J. Poyntz

London the 15th day of August 1663.

To the right Worshippfull Sir Henry Herbert Knight at his house in Ripsford neere Budely in Worcestershire.

## XXXV. LICENSE FOR THE USE OF A SHOVELBOARD[1]

By Vertue of His Majesties Letters Pattents granted unto John Lloyd Gentleman to be Clerke Comptroller of the Revels in England and elsewhere; and by Assignment of the said place unto me by Deputation, and by virtue of the same, I have Examined, Inrolled, and Approved of Thomas Rogers in the Parish of White Chapple to make use of one Shovelbord and no other For the Moderate Exercise and Recreation of Civill Persons Such as the Statute Lawes Allowes of and none other and this to Continue for the space of one whole yeere After the date hereof and noe longer And to the intent the said Thomas Rogers should not intrench upon the Laws and Liberties of His Majesty, or His Powers and Dominions, he hath given security. In testimony hereunto I set my Hand and Seal this        day of 166      And in the fifteenth yeere of his Maiesties Raigne.

J. Poyntz.

---

[1] Halliwell-Phillipps, *Collection*, p. 61. Possibly this is the ' blank' referred to in the preceding letter.

## XXXVI.  HAYWARD'S PROPOSALS TO SIR EDWARD NICHOLAS [1]

To moue Sir Edward Nicholas to write to one of the Secretaries of State, about the following Concernment.

Edward Hayward, gentleman, Deputie to Sir Henry Herbert' Knight, Master of his Majestys Office of the Reuells, finding by some monethes experience and observation, that the validitie and power of that office is much enervated and weakned by the many yeares forced absence of the royall authority, insoemuch that hee concludes it impossible to recover the lost power anciently belonging, and proper to the Master of the Reuells, vnles his gracious Majesty shalbe pleased to grant a warrant for maintaining and reuiuing the respect and dignitie of the office; it is the humble suit of the said Edward Hayward, that his Majesty may bee moued touching the premisses, for an especiall warrant as to the particulars following, in order to a right settlement.

1. To enioyne all Magistrates and whom els it may concerne, to render Due obedience to all Commissions that shalbe granted from the said office, according to ancient custome, and the tenour of the Patent, and vpon their Dissobedience of his Majestys prerogatiue royall in that particular from good testimonialls, that the said Edward Hayward may haue power to send a messenger for them from his Majestys Office of the Reuells, to answere theire contempt, before the right honourable Edward Earle of Manchester, Lord Chamberleine of his Majestys household.

2. That hee, the said Edward Hayward, may haue such further power touching offenders, and refractory persons, as was granted to Geruase Price, Esquire, Sergeant trumpett, by his Majestys warrant bearing date the 7th of October, 1662.

3. That hee may enioy all ancient priuiledges at Court, the ordering of maskes in the Innes of Law, halls, houses of great personages, and societies, all Balls, Dancing schooles, and musick, except his Majestys and the priuiledges of the Corporation touching freemen, if it extend soe farre; Pageantry and other publique tryumphes, the rurall feasts commonly called Wakes, where there is constantly revelling and musick; Cockpitts, fencing and fencing schooles, nocturnall feasts and banquettings in publique houses, when attended with minstrelsy, singing &

[1] Halliwell-Phillipps, *Collection*, p. 59.

Dancing, together with the ordering of all mommeries, fictions, Disguises, scenes and masking attire, all which (in the iudgment of an able Lawyer) are within the verge and comprehension of the Master of the Reuells Patent, from the words Jocorum, Reuelorum et Mascorum.

E. Hayward.

From his Majestys Office of the Revells in St. Pauls churchyard. 26th October. 1663.

My humble proposalls to Sir Edward Nicholas.

## XXXVII. HAYWARD TO SIR HENRY HERBERT[1]

Honourd Sir

I am vnder many discouragementes at present, having paid 226*li* and received only 70*li* from the beginning of my busines to this day, 50*li* I reckoned to receiue from Mister Poyntz, and resolued to pay it to you at the end of November last, but his domineering carriage was such in the office, that I was constrayned rather to part with him then to comply vpon vnreasonable tearmes such as would not bee pleasing either to yourself or mee, by which meanes I am forced to Disappoint you and humbly begge your patience for a time, and rather then giue offence I will pay interest for the forbearance, not Doubting but that I shalbe reimbursed and encouraged when the busines is in a more setled way, and that the royall oake Lotteries, and musick are reduced to obedience, wherein I hope to haue your vtmost furtherance.

Sir, I make it my work and study to improue every thing to the best aduantage, and I hope ere long to reape the fruits of my endeavours. In the meane time I begge your tender regard, however as money comes in it shalbe secured for you in the hands of Mister Baker.

Thus presenting my service to yourself and my Lady, I remaine, worthy Sir

Your most humble servant

E. Hayward.

From the office, the 21th December, 1663.

To the right Worshipfull Sir Henry Herbert Knight, these present.

[1] Halliwell-Phillipps, *Collection*, p. 58.

## XXXVIII. THE OFFICE OF THE REVELS AND THOMAS KILLIGREW[1]

*The heads of what I gave to Mr. Tho. Killegrew*
*the 29th of March, 1664.*

1. To have a generall warrant for musick throughout England, which is practised already, but many are very obstinate, and refuse to take lycences, especially in cities and townes corporate, under the pretence of being freemen.

2. There being many complaints of abuses in dancing schooles, for want of a due inspection and regulation, an order is desired (as it is a most proper branch of the Revells) that I may bee impowered to lycence all the dancing schooles, and to bind them respectively against *mixt* dancing in the schooles, and other practises, which at present begette a scandalous report of them.   This work is already began, and submitted to by some; but it cannot bee done generally, unles countenanced by regall authority.

3. Touching wakes or rurall feasts, (another proper branch of the Revells,) which are annually observed in the greatest part of England, it is humbly desired, that some countenance may be putt upon the lycencing of them, by which means many disorders may bee prevented; and though there bee but 10s. from the most eminent towns, and 5s. from the meaner parishes, (to bee paid annually by the churche wardens,) it will not only bee a good advancement to the office of the Revells, but will much civilize the people, who are commonly disordered at those feasts, which are constantly attended with revelling and musick.

4. All quack salvers and empyrickes, under the denomination of mountebankes, are properly belonging to the Revells, but will not come in (notwithstanding several summons') untill compelled by regall authority.

5. The royall oake lottery, which is a modell or dumb shew, and sortition, and as cleerly belonging to the Revells as the small lottery or pricking book, which have (*ab antiquo*) been commissioned by the office, the persons herein concerned are obstinate, and will not come in, unless compelled by his Majestie's authority.

6. For gaming, though the justices throughout England (amongst other things) bind the victuallers in recognizances of £20 apiece not to tolerate gaming in their houses; yet, nevertheless, under their noses, and to the knowledge of most justices,

---

[1] Rebecca Warner, *Epistolary Curiosities*, Appendix, No. 5, p. 185.   Presumably this was written by Edward Hayward; see paragraph 7.

gaming is sett up and tolerated. Now in regard it is against
the letter of the law to lycence gaming, (though to do the same
is consistent with the Master of the Revells' patent,) it is desired,
with some cautious lymitation, that his Majesty would countenance this particular, as to the lycencing all upon easy termes,
by which meanes every victueller may bee bound to observe
lawfull seasons, and good orders, otherwise it will become a
common custome to play on fast days, in time of divine service,
and at other seasons prohibited; and therefore some expedient
to bee used that may please his Majesty, and support the power
of the Revells, which hath been very much enervated and
weakened by the late times of trouble and distraction.

7. Though to grant lycences for gaming hath been practised
ever since his Majesty's happy returne, by the groome porter,
and Poyntz, yet as to my particular, (who have not enjoyed the
employment above nine months,) I doe act under many feares,
and with much tenderness, to those few who have submitted,
least I should offend the law of the land; and therefore once
againe humbly desire that some safe expedient may bee found
out to reconcile the law and the King's prerogative.

## XXXIX. HAYWARD TO JOHNSON [1]

Mister Johnson

When you see Sir Henry Herbert, present my humble
service to him, and acquaint him that it is onely want of money,
that protracts my waiting on him; with some odde Dribletts
received in 6 weekes time, I haue onely beene enabled to quitt
the rent of my office, and to discharge the stationer for parch-
ment, paper, &c. That soe soone as money comes in, that
may encourage mee to see his face, I shalbe sure to attend vpon
him, but I am vnder soe many discouragements and soe hopeles
of my expectations, that I should reckon it the happiest dayes
work that ever I made in this world to bee quitt of Sir Harry
and the office; the hopes I had by musick is quite lost, I haue
beene cheated of money vpon 3 prizes, haue 30*li.* in debts and
cannot receive one farthing; represent this, and lett the issue
bee what it will, I must stand to it, but at the rate that I haue

[1] Halliwell-Phillipps, *Collection*, p. 60.

observed, I am confident with court allowances and all, it will never amount to 500*li*. a yeare

I am Your Loving friend

E. Hayward.

11th June, 1664.

This ffor Mister George Johnson, at the Lam tavern at the backside of Saint Clemons Church.

Hayward To Johnson. deliuer[ed] to me by Johnson the 13. June 1664.

## XL.  ROUGH ACCOUNTS,  1663–1664[1]

| | | |
|---|---|---|
| Mihelmas. 63 | ...................... | 163. |
| Christmas. 63 | ..................... | 163. |
| Lady day. 64 | ....................... | 163. |
| Midsomer. 64 | ................. | 163. |
| Mihelmas. 64 | ..................... | 163. |

815.

| | | |
|---|---|---|
| 815 | Whereof payd...... | 142. |
| 305 | | |
| — | ⎰ 260 | 673. |
| 510 | ⎱ 250 | |
| 250 | — | 815 |
| | 510 | |

Deducte out of .673. the sume of....... 252.

And Remaines.................. 421.

673.

| | |
|---|---|
| 142 | 142 |
| 163 | 163 |

305 Deducte 305 out of 652.

Re. 347.

And remainder 305.

252 out of 347       652.

---

[1] Halliwell-Phillipps, *Collection*, p. 46.

For 5 quarters at 163 the quarter . . . . . . . . . . 815

       Receiud . . . . . . . . . . . . . . . . . 305.
       Allowed . . . . . . . . . . . . . . . . . 250.

                          555. ⎰
                          260. ⎱

                          815.

       423
       163

             260
305           163

             423
  292   4
   29  10
   16  10
    5  10 charged on Theiter.
 [29  10][1]
 [16  10][1]

 343   4
  14  00 charged on Peinter.
   1  15 From Aris Owinge.
   4  00 On Bucace.
   3  00 On Harmer.
  50  00 more on Izard.

 [65  19][1]
 415  19
  72  11  6

 488  10  6

[1] These figures erased in the original.

Nouember 3. 1663.  Floras Figarys.[1]

| | |
|---|---|
| A Pastorall called ⎱ .................... | 2. |
|    the Exposure ⎰ .................... | 2. |
| 8. more............................ | 16. |
| A Revived Play[2]..................... | 1. |
| Henry the 5th....................... | 2. |
| Revived Play Taminge the Shrew....... | 1. |
| The Generall........................ | 2. |
| Parsons Wedinge..................... | 2. |
| Revived Play.  Mackbethe............. | 1. |
| Henry 8.  Revived Play.............. | 1. |
| House to be let[3]..................... | 2. |
| More for Playes whereof Eluira the last... | 9. |

For Playes......................... 41.


## XLI.  SIR HENRY HERBERT TO THE EARL OF MANCHESTER [4]

*Mill Bridge, Westminster, July 15, 1669.*

My Lord,—The bearer hereof, Anthony Devotte, informs me that Mr. Price, the sergeant trumpett, demandes of him twelve pence a day as due to him from every player; whereas Devotte is not in the notion of a player, but totally distinct from that quality, and makes shewe of puppettes only by virtue of his Majestie's commission, granted to the Master of the Revells under the greate seale, for the authorizing of all publique shewes. And the said serjeant ought not to impose upon the said Devotte, and putt him to great trouble and charges, but should have proceeded legally against him in case he had refused to pay what was legally due.  But the serjeant having arrested Devotte upon his pretended clayme of twelve pence a day, and declared against him, was nonsuited for not proceedinge, which is a matter

---

[1] The portion of this document from here to the end was reproduced by Malone, *Var.* iii. 276.  After "Floras Figaries" he adds "£2."  Halliwell-Phillipps has, incorrectly, it seems, placed two payments of £2 after the next entry.

[2] Malone: "A new play."  That "A Revived Play" is correct is shown by the fee charged.

[3] Probably Davenant's *Playhouse to be Let;* cf. *Var.* iii. 139.

[4] Rebecca Warner, *Epistolary Curiosities*, p. 74.  The Earl of Manchester was the Lord Chamberlain.

of great vexation to a stranger, and a stronge argument against
the validity of the sergeantes grante. Your Lordship, therefore,
is humbly entreated on behalf of the said Devotte to appointe
a day and houre when he shall attende your Lordship with his
counsell, to be hearde before he be concluded in your Lordship's
judgement. And that he may have the benefit of the law for his
protection against the Sergeante's unjust demandes. This from
your Lordship's very humble servant,

HENRY HERBERT.

To the Right Hon. Edward Earle of Manchester, Lord Chamberlayne of his Majestie's houshold.


## XLII. REQUEST FOR A LICENSE FOR DURDIN AND PELLERIN TO SHOW A WOODEN HORSE[1]

A Mylord St. Alban grand Chamberlan.

Supplient humblement François Durdon et André Pellerin
François de Nation disant que de puis quelque temps jl a esté
establi vne Machine en France et particulierement a Versailles
par la quelle on court la bague artiffreictement sur des Chevaux
de bois, Et comme cet establissement ne regarde que la satisfaction du public, ce consideré Mylord Il vous plaise permettre
Aux supplians de le faire en ceste ville de Londres, Et attendu
quil ne se peut qu'a grands frais, et pour leur donner moyen de
se rembourser des depences quil leur conuiendra faire Il vous
plaise aussy Mylord faire deffences a toutes autres personnes de
faire ou jmiter la dite Machine durant le temps de trois Années
a peyne de cinq cent liures sterlins damande et de tous despens
dommages et jnteretz.

Monsieur Durdin for a lycence to shew a wooden horse
French Ambassadors Secretary

[1] Halliwell-Phillipps, *Collection*, p. 99. There is no date given but the Earl of St. Albans was created Lord Chamberlain in 1674.

# INDEX

Abington, *see* Habington.

Activity, feats of, 123.

Adams, Joseph Quincy, 33 *n.* 7, 42 *n.* 1, 46 *n.* 3, 63 *n.* 4, 65 *n.* 1, 66 *n.* 2, 4, 77 *n.* 1, 119 *n.* 2.

*Aglaura*, 76, 118.

*Aglaura the Tragicall Way*, 118.

Albemarle, George Monk, 1 Duke of, 83, 84.

*Alchemist, The*, 44, 49, 117.

*Alcimedon*, 61 *n.* 8.

*Alcimedor*, 61.

*Alexias, or The Chaste Gallant*, 37 *n.* 2.

*Alexis the Chaste Gallant, or The Bashful Lover*, 37 *n.* 2.

*Alexius*, 37 *n.* 2.

*Alexius, or The Chaste Lover*, 37 *n.* 2, 38.

*Alfonso*, 75.

*Alice and Alexis*, 37 *n.* 2.

Allen (a fencer), 47.

*All's Lost by Lust*, 117.

*Alphonso*, 75.

*Alphonsus, Emperor of Germany*, 75.

Amphitheatre, the projected, 46 *n.* 3.

*Angel King, The*, 29.

*Antipodes, The*, 118.

Arber, Edward, 40.

*Arcadia, The*, 30.

*Argalus and Parthenia*, 117.

Aris, 137.

*Arviragus and Philicia*, 55, 56, 57, 75, 76.

Ashborne, Edward, 74.

Ashley, Sir John, *see* Astley.

Astley, Sir John (Master of the Revels), granted reversion of Revels, 7, 103, 104, 109, 110 *n.* 1, 111; becomes Master, 8; commission of powers issued to, 6 *n.* 1; requests allowance for lodging, 71; granted power to protect from arrest, 74 *n.* 2; sells the Office to Herbert, 8, 10, 122; technically the Master until his death, 8 *n.* 3; death of, 102, 109; his Office Book quoted, 48, 49.

Aubigny, Lord, 71, 112.

Aunay, Josias d', 61.

*Baiting of the Jealous Knight, The*, see *The Fair Foul One*.

Baker, 133.

Baldwin, Christopher, 102.

*Ball, The*, 19, 34.

Ballads, licensing of, 125, 127, 128.

Balls, licensing of, 132. ║

Banquets, licensing of, 133.

Barber, of playhouse, 99.

*Barnavelt, The Tragedy of Sir John van Olden*, 18.

Barnes (playwright), *The Madcap*, 28.

Bartholomew Fair, 127.

*Bartholomew Fair*, 117.

Bartley, Sir William, *Cornelia*, 118.

*Bashful Lover, The*, 37.

Basse, Mrs. (the law-woman), 56.

Basse, Thomas, 63.

Batterton, Thomas, *see* Betterton.

Beale, 130.

Beaumont, Francis, *see* Fletcher, John.

*Beauties, The*, 34.

Beaver, show of a live, 46.

Beaver, Michael, 111.

Beeston, Christopher, promises to reform a play, 19; makes payment to Herbert, 35; as manager of the Cockpit, pays £60 annually to Herbert, 45, 101; yields the Cockpit to the French players, 61; commanded to make a company of boys, 66; gives Herbert's wife a pair of gloves, 67; *see also* William Beeston, *and* Beeston's Boys.

Beeston, William, 66, 81, 105, 111, 121.

Beeston's Boys (at the Cockpit in Drury Lane), organized, 66; act play at Court, 57, 58; inhibited, 66; other actors forbidden to use their plays, 64 *n.* 1.

*Beggar's Bush, The*, 49, 75, 77, 82, 116.

*Beginning of the World, The*, 47 *n.* 5.

*Believe as You List*, 19 *n.* 2, 31 *n.* 3, 33.

*Bellman of Paris, The*, 24.

Benefit performances, for authors, 67; for the Master of the Revels, 43–45, 101, 106, 121.

Benfielde, Robert, 21, 44 *n.* 1, 64.

Benger, Sir Thomas (Master of the Revels), 4, 110 *n.* 1.

Berkeley, Sir William, *The Lost Lady*, 76, 117.

Betterton, Thomas, articles of agreement with Davenant, 96–100, 106;

140